NO MORE
CLOUDY DAYS

For ordering Information or quantity discounts:
Daniel Berry
1031 Martha's Way
Conyers, GA 30013
PH- 678-977-2298
dan@southcoastal.org

www.facebook.com/nomorecloudydays

Cover Design:
Jeanette Berry

Classic Publishing
www.classicpublishing.net

CLASSIC
PUBLISHING
Dover, Delaware

NO MORE
CLOUDY DAYS

The bend in the road
is not the end of the road!

DANIEL A. BERRY

Table of Contents

Dedication   i
Foreword   ii
Introduction   iii
Chapter 1   Living in the Land of Blessing   1
Chapter 2   Life Can Change Forever in a Second   13
Chapter 3   I Believe We Can Make It   31
Chapter 4   When Faith Doesn't Make Sense   47
Chapter 5   Adjusting to the New Normal   65
Chapter 6   Starting on the Path of Healing   85
Chapter 7   Two Steps Forward One Step Back   101
Chapter 8   Looking for a Higher Purpose   115
Chapter 9   Understanding Grief   127
Chapter 10   Permission to Get Unstuck   143
Chapter 11   Lessons Learned on My Journey   157
Chapter 12   No More Cloudy Days   173
Small Group Guidelines   190
Biographical Information   192
Selected Bibliography   193

Dedication

I am forever indebted to my family who has stood with me through this journey. When others run away, thank God my family ran toward me and loved us with unconditional love.

I am forever indebted to my district family called *South Coastal District of The Wesleyan Church*. Thank you for your patience during some lean years of personal leadership. I hung on as your district leader but it was your prayer, patience, and love that enabled me to negotiate those rough waters. Without your generosity this book could have never been written.

I am thankful for Kimberly Kirkland for those early creative edits and suggestions. Thank you Chet Todd, who helped me write and edit those difficult personal chapters. Without your encouragement to relive "my story" this book would never have been completed. And most of all, to my precious son Joshua Berry who decided to help his dad on the final difficult edits of the book. *We did it together!*

Thank you to my Mom and Dad who lived this journey as close as anyone could. You were by my side encouraging and praying throughout the entire journey.

And thank you Shelley Berry for your life, love, and legacy that you have left for your children and grandchildren. Hopefully one day they will read this book and see that we kept the faith and finished our course well.

And thank you Debbie Berry for saying, "Dan, you have to finish that book so God can give you closure." You pushed me to complete this project and tell our story for our families to read in generations to come.

And for those of you who kept saying, "*You ought to write a book,*" you were my worst nightmare and my best encouragers! May God use this book to help someone who is at the end of their rope hang on a little longer! And may God give you hope and comfort in the reading of these words.

i

Foreword

Eighty four years is a long time to live. I have asked God many times over the past decade why He would leave me here so long. I think I now know – to help my son and his wife with one of life's biggest battles. There is no one else that could have helped Dan and Shelley fight this battle except my wife and me. Retirement does have its advantages. In these last years, God gave Ann and me a mission and we would do it all over again if we could!

Over the next twelve chapters you are going to read a story that will seem horrific and beyond comprehension. When I read the first draft I cried, laughed, and relived every twist of the journey. My wife and I lived the story beside my first born son. I saw him face each one of these crisis. I did my best to pick him up when he was discouraged and I rejoiced with him and Shelley at every step forward. Several times we thought that Shelley was going to fight back to some form of normal but each time we were disappointed.

I kept telling Dan that God had another chapter in the book of his life. This book represents that next chapter of God's hand of providence. I can't believe he actually finished writing this story and it is going to print. I know how hard it was for him to relive the story of this journey.

Dan wrote this book to help turn his crisis into a story of bulldog perseverance and God's redemptive power. I hope from the bottom of my heart that God will use this book to bless your life. I pray it will also help Dan use what was meant for evil to be used for the glory of God and the salvation of others.

Lastly, I also pray that God will use this book to encourage you and help everyone know that you "can smile again" even if it looks impossible today.

Weldon Atwood Berry

Introduction

Every journey in life starts with the first step. The book you are holding in your hand has been started at least five different times. Every time I began to write I had to rest my pen and stop writing. Reliving the drama of this story was emotionally overwhelming. Reviewing the daily journal entries in Caring Bridge was so painful that I had to retreat from the memory of the journey. It would place me in depression for days after writing the story. This story you are about to read has finally been completed after numerous attempts and abundance of help from friends.

This book is not for the faint of heart or for those looking to read a story about miracles every minute, fairy tale endings, and neat bowed conclusions. If you are looking for a story with raw emotions, real life challenges, and a story of tenacity - this is your book! It is a real story with human struggles, frailties, and pain. But it is also a book filled with real life answers developed through the crucible of life's toughest journey. It finds its center in a faith in God, old fashion commitment to the marriage vows, and dependency on God's generous grace. Sometimes in real life it is a big "win" to just hold on and survive.

It is also written for men; for men who take a vow for "better or worse." Few of us ever consider the possibility of the "worse". When we dream, we dream about the fulfillment of the highest and noblest dreams. But what do you do when your dreams crumble? How do you dig down deep and keep a vow to your spouse and family in the middle of unthinkable circumstances? How do you live and maintain your character when you are under unbelievable pressure? This book answers those questions and more!

Lastly it was written as a therapeutic attempt to help me and others like me. It was personally helpful to chronicle the story and be reminded of how God brought me through. Sometimes it is not easy to see God when you are in the darkness of the night. It is my hope that I can use my pain to help others who are facing their own grief and "dark night of the soul." So, this book was written to give a little light of hope to someone on a similar journey who may be crying out in desperation and all they hear is deafening silence. The title came to me from two separate parts of this story. The title whirled around in my head for weeks and then a personal friend said, "Dan, why not add a subtitle that can explain the full story." So the subtitle was born to give clarity. There is an old gospel song called "Uncloudy Days" by Josiah Atwood. It says, "*O they tell me of a home far beyond the skies, O they tell me of a home far away; O they tell me of a home where no storm clouds rise, O they tell me of an unclouded day.*" And for every Christian it is our blessed hope to be with Jesus. But there is another song with a similar title that is not gospel but secular written by Glenn Fry. The song says in one stanza, "*I know a place where we can go where true love always stays. There's no more stormy nights, no more cloudy days.*" It too tells the story of the journey and captures the essence of trying to live through brokenness and find life and love again.

The best news yet is that our soul cry for "no more cloudy days" is ultimately fulfilled one day in heaven and in Jesus. Within every human soul there is a deep cry for something more than this life. A place where there is no more pain, loss, and suffering. And a place where there really is no more cloudy days. - Dan

Living in the Land of Blessing

Chapter 1 Living in the Land of Blessing

"From the fullness of his grace we have all received one blessing after another." John 1:16 NIV

""I'm so blessed with a great family, and I've had success in my career" Michael J. Fox

"Blessed is the man who makes the LORD his trust. . ." Ps 40:4 – NIV

"I've seen better days, but I've also seen worse. I don't have everything I want, but I do have all I need. I woke up with some aches and pains, but I woke up. My life may not be perfect, but I am blessed." - Unknown

It was a hot, sweltering August Saturday in Conyers, Georgia. My wife Shelley and I had spent most of the morning mowing the grass, pulling weeds and making the yard look as sharp as the polished grass of the White House lawn. We both loved to work outside. Whether it was the heat of the summer or a beautiful fall day, we loved being close to nature. Anytime we had a day off we would gladly choose to unwind by working around the house and make the place look as nice as possible.

After hours of work, and with the yard now looking perfect for the weekend, I took time for some much rest. I was relishing the moment sitting on those white brick steps, surrounded by our front porch, I relished the moment. Shelley knew how to make a moment like this more enjoyable. Unknown to me, she had been inside fixing my summer favorite; cold iced tea. She came out with two large glasses and said, "Dan let's take a break". With sweat pouring down my face and clothes dripping with perspiration we sat down together on the front porch.

Every couple has those moments when it seems life stands still; a moment permanently imprinted in the mind. This was one of those moments; one truly made for eternity. As we sat and talked, we chatted about our many blessings; our kids, our past, and our future. Looking over the front yard we marveled at God's grace that allowed us to purchase this beautiful property. God had given us a home valued at least fifty thousand more than we had paid. It was a miracle story of God's provision!

We talked about the day when our grandchildren would play in the backyard. We dreamed about playgrounds, go carts, battery driven cars, kid's toys, and family memories yet to happen. In that moment, life was serene; the hard work was behind us, the lawnmower no longer drowned out our conversation. It was just the two of us enjoying the company of each other. We were sharing one of those beautiful moments in life that couples who have spent almost thirty years together appreciate.

"Dan," Shelley said, "we have been so blessed". I acknowledged her comment as I took another long drink of the cool ice tea. "We have had such a wonderful life," she continued. "We have two godly boys and two wonderful daughters-in-law. How much better can it get?" We reflected for a while on the many blessings God had given us. We also chatted about the news we had received only days before of our first grandchild on the way. Both of us knew God had been so good to us throughout our lives.

We recalled our ministry together for the last twenty-five years. Our first pastorate was in New Castle, Pennsylvania. A sleepy little western Pennsylvania town filled with rusty old steel mill factories and century old homes. It was known for its great hot dogs and rusty retired factories. There was a hot dog stand on almost every city block. They told me when I accepted the call to pastor their church that the community consumed more hot dogs per capita than any place in the world. While I served that little church I learned it was probably true. It was my first senior pastor position after leaving United Wesleyan College in Allentown, PA. I remember Dr. Earle Wilson, my mentor, telling me that I could have done far better if I would have just waited. We followed the heart of God and accepted the call. They chose me and I chose them; a small group of twenty-five struggling Christians in a near dead congregation. They loved us and promised to follow if we would lead (they meant it too). We lead, sacrificed, took risks, and we reached new people and the church grew. They became like family. They loved us, loved our family, and worked with us. We look back now and realize that little church was the birthplace of Shelley and my ministry together. Both our boys were born in that city hospital. And I will never forget eating chili hot dogs to celebrate while Shelley was in labor. I have so many fond and wonderful memories of God's blessing in that place.

As we continued to reminisce, the tone of the conversation changed. Shelley became serious and seemed concerned about the future. She had always cared so much about our being able to spend many years together in retirement. "Dan, I want you to take care of yourself," she said. "I want us to retire and live long lives together. Please take care of yourself." Then she spoke the words that penetrated my conscience. "Don't you go and leave me." Her serious comment puzzled me. "Shelley, I would never leave you." Then I began to realize exactly what she meant.

Once you reach the age of fifty it seems the body begins to sag and the pounds begin to stick. I had become lax in my eating habits and had gained excess weight. My health was beginning to slip and I was not exercising as I had in previous days. I had allowed the stress of my job to push me to unhealthy levels of living. When some people get under pressure they stop eating. Others simply use food as a way to cope. I looked her in the eyes with resolve and said, "Shelley, I'm going to get healthier this fall. Things will slow down and I'll have more time for both of us to get back to walking, consistent exercise, and eating better." We both agreed that we would do better in the future.

At that moment I meant every word of my vow. I did intend to get healthier. I wanted so much to live a long life with our

3

kids and future grandkids. I wanted with all my heart to grow old with Shelley. In that moment we glanced into a hopeful future and anticipated the birth of our first grandchild.

I rested a little while longer then returned to mowing the grass. We placed all the equipment back in the shed, and life moved on as usual that Saturday afternoon. That fifteen minute conversation, however, would be forever chiseled into my memory as the words, "Dan, don't you go and leave me!" echoed in my mind.

When you look back over your life, how do you rate it? Is it one of blessing after blessing or somewhere on the other end of the spectrum toward difficulty after despair? Most of us in America are blessed beyond comprehension. I have traveled abroad to third world countries and know how blessed we are. A few years ago a Christian leader in Jamaica said to me, "In America you look to heaven as a great place of gold, silver, tranquility and peace. The people of Jamaica look at America the same way you look at heaven." When you leave our borders it doesn't take long to realize that we live in a blessed nation. Even those who claim that status of poverty are better off economically than millions in other parts of the world. In this nation we are blessed beyond what we deserve!

As far back as I can remember I have been taught the value of being thankful for the blessings of life. When I was a child in church we sang the old hymn, "Count your blessings name them one by one." I've found when you start counting those blessings you soon realize that the blessings are innumerable. I was raised in a godly family. My mom and dad are still married today in their 80's. I have been able to have a good education! I am blessed beyond what I deserve!

Every family has its own memorable traditions. Our family has developed many over the last thirty years. One in particular that has always linked our family together is expressing thankfulness. It may seem a little strange to some, but when we get together

4

for special holiday gatherings like Thanksgiving or Christmas we always close our time with a circle of prayer and thankfulness.

This family ritual looks something like this, just before the car pulls out of the driveway, we gather outside and hold hands. We stand facing each other in a circle. Usually the senior male of the family takes the lead. If my dad were present he would start things off. After saying our "goodbyes" we pray together; always focusing on God's amazing blessing to our family, His provisions and protection. We close repeating this simple statement: "Father we thank you for this moment and we realize that we may never gather together like this again as a family." New members to the family often comment that the prayer time is a tad bit morbid. But it's true! You never know when you'll ever have another "family moment" like we are having at that moment. Moments in life are never repeatable so we cherish every opportunity God provides.

For some reading this you may be smiling or frowning, but it is our tradition and it is biblical! And for us it is a constant reminder not to take the blessings of God lightly. My father always taught our family that every moment we are together as a family is a sacred moment in time. We may never have the same people around that circle in the same way as in that moment. If you haven't discovered, life is very fragile! So every time we gather we remember that all that is good could disappear in an instant. The next gathering is not guaranteed by God.

Over the years we have been surrounded by so many who have been hurt deeply by the loss of family members and loved ones. James 4:14 reminds us that we do not have clue about what will happen tomorrow, "For what is your life? It is even a vapor that appears for a little time and then vanishes away." Understanding this biblical truth, we have kept it as a focal point among our family values.

I often thought of my aging mom and dad who in spite of health challenges were growing older and were now in their 80's.

We knew that eventually the day would come when we would receive the news that they had gone on to heaven. This realization caused us to be thankful for God's blessings but at the same time keep one eye focused on the reality of life. Time is a fragile gift from God we have been given and we are never guaranteed tomorrow. What we do with the moments we have affect so deeply how we face the difficult moments ahead.

Up until September 10, 2007 our family had been living in the land of blessing and favor. Many of the illness and problems that most people face in life had escaped us. We constantly acknowledged that God was the reason for our blessing and I don't believe we took His promise lightly. My Dad wouldn't have allowed that to happen to our family.

So, let me ask you a question I have thought many times. Is there a danger in living such a blessed life of thinking that it will never be any different? Deep down inside I think so! Too many people operate with the belief that by constantly giving God praise for His protection they are exempt from problems and tragedy. We know intellectually that the "rain falls on the just and unjust", so it must stand to reason that "tragedy falls on the just and unjust". But I believe that it is possible that when you live a consistent life of abundant blessing it can lead to presumption. Presuming that it may happen to those "other families" but it won't happen to our family. Thinking that if we just give God thanks, keep living our lives for Him, then we will be spared crisis.

I'm not talking about sinful, arrogant, presumption that your plans for life will unfold without a glitch. Most of us allow for, and even anticipate, small trajectory changes in the course of our life. Somewhere deep down inside however, we might lull ourselves into believing that, no matter what happens, God's grace will make all things right; that we are favored among all His children. We might presume that because we are "good" people and have done some many wonderful things for God that we will miss out on those tragic stories that others share.

6

What I'm talking about are the earth shaking changes we never see coming; those crisis moments that happen to other people and not us; the unexpected events that wake us up to the fact that sometimes the path God has planned is different than the course we have charted for ourselves.

One of our first great physical crises came to our family in March of 2007. Shelley drove to her gynecologist in Covington for her annual breast examination. Within a few days the doctor's office called us back with the report that there was an abnormality. This had happened before so neither of us was deeply concerned. Many times those abnormalities turn out to only be a glitch in the x-ray machine or the x-ray operator. After a second exam and several more x-rays, however, the doctor recommended a lumpectomy. Now, we were living in uncharted territory!

Within a week Shelley was in the Newton General Hospital in Covington, GA for the operation. This time the news was not good. The lumpectomy had revealed a trace of cancer. The "C" word can cause chills to run up and down your spine. Shelley's mom had undergone a mastectomy a few years earlier and that dreaded "C" word had always been a fear for Shelley. I believe most women fear a mammogram for this very reason: the possibility of hearing that you have cancer.

After the surgery the doctor informed us there were several options available. Shelley could take the radical option of a mastectomy or pursue a less radical option of radiation. We asked the doctor for his advice. After much prayer by family and friends we decided to go the less radical route. This would mean thirty three treatments of radiation over a six to eight week period. Then, it would be followed by regular medication to assure us that it would not return.

We had taken the news of cancer as a battle of faith and now we would view the treatment in the same way. I was always confident that Shelley was going to do extremely well. Each day I left early from work and took Shelley to the doctor for her treatments. I wanted to be part of the healing at least emotionally. We established our routine and the weeks passed without incident. We were confident that God would bring us though this crisis and our faith would sustain us throughout the entire ordeal.

The last day of treatment was a Monday. I remember it vividly. Sunday had been a busy day of travel so we both slept in to get some much needed rest. We awoke, showered, dressed and prepared for her last day of treatment. By the time of her appointment Shelley was showing signs of getting weaker. Her energy level had dropped but she was doing amazing. This was celebration day; the last day of treatment!

We drove to the treatment with such exhilaration and joy. We anticipated getting a good report and the thought of having no more treatments to endure brought excitement. We were so happy to get this routine behind us. We felt that this was going to be one of the best days of our life. Our hope was confirmed with good news. After the examination and the final x-ray she was pronounced cancer free. After a long period of indecision, uncertainty and trial, there were new days dawning. I cannot describe for you the joy of leaving that doctor's office. The birds seemed to be chirping louder and the sky did not have one cloud. It was a wonderful day when we could once more say we are blessed.

Shelley had been a real trooper. This trial had only served to strengthen her faith. For days, unknown to Shelley, I had been planning a very special celebration. This was of course her "graduation" day and what a day I had planned! We left the doctors and I let her in on the little surprise.

Originally, I had planned to take her to the Blue Willow Restaurant in Social Circle, Georgia. It was one of her favorite restaurants and a place where many great family memories had occurred. However, I found out a few days before that the restaurant was closed on Mondays, so we headed for the Olive Garden in Lithonia, Georgia; her second favorite place.

There was one stop I wanted to make before the restaurant. We pulled into The Man's Store (aka Sam's Club). A few days earlier, I had spied a beautiful necklace made of mother of pearl. If you know anything about pearls you know they have an awesome symbolic story of turning irritation into something good. The idea of giving a gift of pearls was to be one of those lingering lessons of tenacity and faith.

Pearls are formed as a result of a defense mechanism often found in living shelled mollusks. A foreign substance, often a parasite or something small that poses a threat to the mollusk becomes lodged in the shell. The mollusk will begin to secrete a smooth calcium layer that hardens around the object, incasing it so that it cannot inflict damage. In essence pearls exist because something initially harmful or painful has been changed into something beautiful and of great value.

To me this was the perfect gift for a lovely woman who had faced the fear of cancer. Her faith had been tested and God had brought her through with a high hand. She had used her story of trial to help other women during their treatment. It was a trophy of victory after a long battle. We were once again living in the land of blessing!

We walked into Sam's hand in hand. I could hardly wait to take her to the jewelry counter. With a big smile on my face I said, "Shelley, I want to get you something special. You can pick anything you want today in the jewelry counter". Secretly, I was hoping she would pick the pearl necklace.

After making her way around the counter several times, we stood looking at the pearl rings, necklaces and pendants. I spoke

9

up and said, "Shelley, what about a pearl necklace? It could be such a testimony of your journey." She has always been such a practical person. Many times in our marriage she could have chosen the more expensive items or the more elaborate gift, but she never did. She always chose the practical gift. It was just one of those things that made Shelley the woman whom I loved.

"Dan, I would rather have a pearl ring rather than a necklace," she said. "I will hardly ever wear a pearl necklace." Again, it was the practical Shelley. So, our focus turned to the ring section. She first looked at a ring with a single pearl, but then carefully decided on the double pearl ring. I even encouraged her to go with two. I was feeling very generous. It was absolutely a gorgeous pick and represented everything I had wanted the choice to be.

Shelley slipped the ring on her finger. I couldn't remember when she had allowed me to purchase such an extravagant gift for her. Tears came to her eyes and her face beamed with pride; pride at what God had brought us through; pride at the thought of what lay ahead; pride in our marriage that had not only weathered this storm of sickness but had been strengthened by it. It was one of those eternal moments. It was a moment I had prayed it would be!

We left Sam's Club and drove to the Olive Garden. After we were seated in a booth, we sat across from each other and just gazed into each other's eyes for a moment. What a long and tiring battle! What a joy to be on the other side. As we ate our lunch we talked heart to heart. She told me how much she loved me! I told her how much I loved her and we both agreed that the trial labeled as cancer was behind us. We were turning from one dark chapter in our lives to a bright and beautiful chapter. Thank God, the storm was past and we had made it through this trial intact.
We left Olive Garden and stopped by the district office to drop off several office supplies I had picked up at Sam's. This gave Shelley a chance to show off the ring to Joan, our office secretary. The fact that she loved it so much thrilled my heart. Leaving the office we headed toward home. The future was bright and life was good. I

picked up my cell phone to call my family to share the news. I handed the phone to her, "Mom Berry, you won't believe what Dan gave me today?" She was sharing the joys of that day and we were once again living in the land of blessing. Nothing could steal the joys of this day! Nothing!

CHAPTER ONE STUDY GUIDE:

1. Discussion: Take a few minutes and reflect on some of the many blessings that you have been given in your life (family, friends, health, job, etc.)? What do the blessings in life say about God and his goodness? Do you take often take note of the small things as well as the large blessings?

2. According to James 1: 16-17 from where do our blessings come?

3. Read James 1:3. How does God "test our faith"? How has God tested you in the past?

4. In John 10:27-28 what are the blessings we receive when we belong to Jesus?

5. What life lessons can you learn through the multiple blessings of God?

6. What is the downside of failing to be thankful for the blessings of God?

7. Have you ever felt so blessed and favored by God that you were invincible?

8. How might you practice the daily discipline of giving God thanks?

PRAYER:

"Lord, you are a good and gracious God. I remember this moment with thankfulness. Thank you for health, family, friends, and blessings. I realize that everything I have and hold will slip away one day. You have given me life. God, I acknowledge that your purpose is not to hurt or harm me but to bless me and make me a blessing. As I have been blessed please help me to be a blessing to those who I will meet today. And help me to cherish the moments! Who knows how quickly they could vanish? In Jesus Name, Amen"

Chapter 2 In a Moment Life Can Change Forever

"My grace is sufficient for you, for my power is made perfect in weakness." Therefore I will boast all the more gladly about my weaknesses, so that Christ's power may rest on me. That is why, for Christ's sake, I delight in weaknesses, in insults, in hardships, in persecutions, in difficulties. For when I am weak, then I am strong."
2 Corinthians 12:7

"God, grant me the serenity to accept the things I cannot change, the courage to change the things I can, and the wisdom to know the difference."
Reinhold Niebuhr

"The Matrix" is a science fiction movie filled with religious and philosophical symbolism. The plot is set many years in the future and supposes that the reality of what we see is a lie. It presents the idea that, in fact, humans live in mechanical, life support vats, while being fed false sensory information by a giant virtual reality computer (the Matrix). The humans of this story are unaware that everything they think is real is simply the creation of a highly advanced computer program. The perpetrators of this horror are intelligent machines who feed on humans as a source of power. Humans are literally farmed. Scary!

The central character of the film is Neo. Neo is presented as a loner who is searching for a mysterious character called Morpheus (named after the Greek god of dreams and sleep). He believes he knows the answer to the question "What is the Matrix?" Morpheus contacts Neo just as the machines (posing as sinister 'agents') are trying to keep Neo from discovering truth. When Morpheus and Neo meet, Morpheus offers Neo two pills. The red pill will answer the question "what is the Matrix?" by removing him from it. If he takes the blue pill, however, life continues as usual. As Neo reaches for the red pill Morpheus warns Neo, "Remember, all I'm offering is the truth. Nothing more." The film as a whole, and especially the scene where Neo must choose between the red and blue pills, is deeply compelling. It begs the question: What would you do given the same choice? If someone came up to you and said, "With one little pill all your deceptions about reality will be removed." Would you take it?

Monday, September 10, 2007 started like a wonderful day, yet for me and my family, this was to be our "red pill" day. On this day my eyes would be opened to a "parallel universe" that existed beside my land of blessing. Up until this day I had been sheltered by the green pastures of blessing. Now, life was about to change and change forever. I had no idea of the journey that lay before me, or the brutal reality I would be catapulted into. You can mark it on your calendar, after that September 10th Monday, my life would never be the same again.

Perhaps you can recall a "red pill" day like that on your calendar? Life was moving along nicely. Bills paid, a good job, a home, a family, a future, and then suddenly life was turned upside down. You may have lost your job, been evicted from your new dream home, and your future forever changed. It could have been the loss of a marriage or solemn news from your doctor. In a heartbeat, you were thrust into a new reality that you neither desired nor expected. That day became a turning point in your life.

That September Monday was a very special day for Shelley and me. We awoke early so Shelley could to go to her last of 33 radiation treatments for breast cancer. Throughout her treatment, Shelley kept a spirit of faith and optimism. Every morning she was up early spending time with God and she was continually talking about this faith journey. What kept her spirits up the most was preparing for her first grandchild who was to be born in October. We were only a few months away from one of the proudest moments in the life of a parent. And no one on the face of planet earth wanted to love, hold, and pamper her grandkids more than Shelley. I really think she was more excited about the birth of this grandbaby than anything imaginable.

We were also excited to be closing the chapter on this phase of life and moving to another better and happier chapter. All morning long we talked about how the treatment had gone just textbook perfect and the tests where showing signs that the original "spot" had disappeared, never to return again. We were once again living in the land of blessing!

Around 1:00 PM we turned left into our housing development called Martha's Vineyard. No, not "that" Martha's Vineyard! As we made the turn, out of nowhere came a small, low profile car racing over the hill at 70 mph or greater. We later learned from eye witnesses that this young man had been weaving in and out of traffic and driving erratically for miles down north on Route 20. Many people had beeped their horns to try to get his attention to "slow down" but without avail. One witness later shared that she had said to herself, "He is going to kill somebody if he doesn't slow down".

We made our left into the development. He seemed to see us and weave into the left lane, as if he was trying to avoid colliding with us. To this day I believe he was attempting to keep the gas pedal to the floor like those action car race movies and dart by us. However, he was going so fast he could not control the vehicle and we had no time to get out of his way. It seemed like time stood still for minutes. "He's going to hit us!" I remember thinking! But that was the last thought I had.

The impact of the two cars colliding was heard around the neighborhood. I was knocked unconscious! When I came to, our car was facing northbound, I was sitting behind the steering wheel, and the air bags had exploded. Someone was in the car, shaking my head and asking, "Mister, are you alright? Are you alright?" I responded quickly, not recognizing the voice and the face. I remember saying, "I'm OK", then looking over I saw Shelley. It was a surreal moment! She was trying desperately to breath and someone was lifting her head to keep her breathing while others were calling on their cell phones trying to quickly get an ambulance. It seemed like hours but it was only a few minutes. I was dazed and numb. This could not be real. It could not be happening to us on this celebration day. It felt like a horrible dream I would awaken from and everything would be alright. I kept crying out, "Please don't worry about me. Just take care of my wife. I'm fine! Please take care of my wife". Over and over again I would say those words throughout the day, "Please take care of my wife!" Somehow I knew I was not seriously hurt but Shelley was in serious condition. There was only a little blood, but it was evident that she was fighting for her life. I couldn't believe I was living this moment in time.

As soon as I stepped out of the accident vehicle, an excruciating pain shot through my groin. In shock I tried to force myself to stand only to fall to the ground. Later, I would learn that I had suffered a broken pelvis from bracing myself on the floorboard of the car with my feet during the impact. My only thought was to help Shelley at all cost, but I could not even stand to get to her. I felt utterly helpless! I was totally dependent upon the good Samaritans who were doing everything they could for her. I simply watched in horror as an unknown man kept her head erect so she could breathe!

People were asking me for my address, phone numbers, and other vital information but I was dazed and in shock. I remember taking my wallet out of my back pocket and literally handing it to a stranger and saying, "it's in there somewhere." They could have taken every dime I had at this moment and I didn't care. My only thought was "Shelley has got to be alright. . . . this can't be happening God. . . . . Oh, God I'm going to awaken out of this nightmare any moment and find it isn't happening!"

All the focus was on Shelley. Someone called the ambulance and within minutes she was whisked away to the parking lot of the nearby Target Department Store. At the parking lot a medivac helicopter was waiting to rush her to Atlanta Medical Center. Time was of the essence if they were to save her life. I knew deep down inside this was not good.

16

I was placed on a stretcher and rushed to the Atlanta Medical Center. That Monday still seems like a blur to me. I can scarcely remember anything about that ride except praying silently for Shelley as I drifted in and out of consciousness. And thinking, "This can't be happening God!" I knew it was very serious but I also believed that things were going to be alright. Somehow, God had always brought us through the most difficult problems and I "knew" this time would be no different. God was going to protect us, just like He always had in the past. Somehow or someway things would work out and life would return to normal after this new crisis.

When my son Jason was just a boy, he rode his bicycle across the road in front of the church in Armbrust, Pa. and was hit by a car. Though he was bumped, bruised, and scared out of his mind, God spared his young life. God had always spared our family. We had near misses like most people but God had always protected us and blessed us. Often we commented on how good He was to keep us from tragedy and death. When you see others go through such tragedy you always are thankful for every moment you have. But now I was living one of those unimaginable moments of life! I was now the unfortunate victim and circumstances were spinning out of our control.

When God's protecting hand is on you so consistently, it's easy to feel like you are exempt from serious crisis. You almost get a feeling of invincibility. It is always the other family and not our family! For most of us though, at some point in our life we wake up to the fact that God's children experience tragedy just like everyone else. Though He loves and cares for us more than we can possibly imagine, He never promised to shield us from the valleys of pain and hardship. He has promised, however, that when we walk through such valleys, He will never leave us. I didn't know it at the time, but that Monday I entered the valley that would wake me up to this truth. It was my "red pill" day!

When I arrived at the Medical Center they wisped me into the emergency room. As I waited for a physician and a diagnosis, I was continually asking everyone who came by the area, "Has anyone heard about the condition of my wife?" No one would say a word and it felt like they were trying to avoid answering my questions. I had been with families in the hospital in moments like these as a pastor and I had learned what absence of information means. I knew in my heart things were bad, but God has always come through for us. I couldn't imagine that things would be different now. "God is too good to fail us in this crisis," I kept thinking. "Shelley is going to make it!"

I looked up and saw three friendly faces: Jason Berry, my son, Dr. Dan Reiland and Dr. Kevin Myers from 12Stone Church near Atlanta. They had heard about the accident and had come to the emergency room to be with my family. Their positive spirit and calm demeanor was such a blessing, but I could sense myself growing more frustrated. No one would tell me anything. "I am not naïve!" I thought. I knew things were not good but I still held fast to an internal crazy hope that things would turn out alright. Despite the fact that I could read the concern on the faces of my son Jason and friends, I just knew God was going to make it work out for good.

It seemed like an eternity before they rolled me down the cold hospital hallway to have X-rays taken. They discovered that I had broken ribs, a broken pelvis and concussion. They admitted me and I was taken to my hospital room. All the while I'm asking questions and getting no response from my family and friends. I could surmise from foggy observation they were trying to protect me from something unpleasant.

Over the next few days family members from around the country either drove or flew in to be with Shelley and me. My son Joshua and his wife Misti drove down from Indianapolis. My brother Michael and his wife Renee from Kansas City shut down his pediatric dental practice to be at our side. My two brothers and their wives, Mark and Debbie, and Steve and Jeanette, were there as well, and of course, my faithful parents from Salisbury, Maryland came as soon as they could drive those twelve long hours. During crisis time it sure is good to have family and friends who know how to pray, encourage, and act on your behalf.

The next few days seemed like a blur as I slowly learned the truth about Shelley's health. The family gathered around me and broke the news to me gently. They told me that she was in intensive care and in a coma. They were hoping that she would awaken any day. She had many internal injuries and the first 48 hours she was hanging on to life by a thread. They would conduct more tests on her brain as soon as she was stable. She was on a respirator because she could not breathe on her own. It was quite serious and I realized that her life hung in the balance.

I lay in the hospital bed feeling helpless and broken. I was in pain from the broken ribs and very cloudy in my thinking. I kept asking the same questions over and over again. Because of my broken pelvis, they ordered me not to put any weight on my feet for at least 8 weeks so the bones could heal. Each night a family member would spend the night in the hospital room with me and try to comfort me from the overwhelming sense of despair and concern.

They did not let me visit Shelley until the second day. On that day my sons Jason and Joshua helped me get into a wheelchair and go down to the emergency room to see Shelley. I was anxious to see my bride and felt as if I could get close to her, I could speak and call her out of her coma. Despite Jason and Joshua's attempts to verbally prepare me for the visit to the intensive care ward, nothing could prepare me for what I was about to see.

When he pushed me in the room I saw a motionless body on a ventilator, hooked up to many tubes and wires. The pumping sound of that ventilator still echoes in my brain to this day. Here was my precious wife and the mother of my children, barely hanging on to life. The sight of such helplessness and vulnerability overwhelmed me and I broke under the sight. Husbands are supposed to protect their wives. We are their champions; their providers; the one they look to for support and safety. Yet here I was sitting in a wheelchair, looking up into my wife's pale face, unable to do anything as she fought to live. This was so foreign to me. In one brief moment I had been ripped out of my familiar world of blessing and thrust into the world of modern medicine and intensive care personnel. I felt so very helpless! I could not even stand to fight this battle. I thought, "This cannot be happening!"

I caressed her hair with my hand and prayed. I just knew God would hear my desperate prayers and was going to awaken her from her coma and she was going to start recovering. Shelley was always a fighter and this challenge would not be too great for her bull dog tenacity. I went back to my room and cried with deep wails from the bottom of my aching soul. I looked out the hospital window, starring into the distant space numb. I was dazed, beaten and broken by the site of such helplessness. For the first time since the accident I was facing a cruel and harsh reality. I realized we were in unchartered waters and in a challenge for the very existence of life as I knew it. Reality was starting to hit me and it was hitting me hard. I thought to myself, "things may never be the same again!"

Within a few days of the accident my family received literally hundreds of calls from friends around the country. My brother Mark wisely started a CaringBridge webpage to answer the questions of so many people who wanted to know, day by day, how she was progressing. To have answered every email or every phone call would have taken a full time employee. Each night Mark and Debbie would write an update about Shelley and me to hundreds of people who signed up to receive the CaringBridge updates. I did not know it at the time but this growing group of prayer-cadres would become the foundation of the prayer. They were foot soldiers that would sustain us in the months to come. I had no idea how faith sustaining this group of prayer warriors would prove to be over time.

We had hope in spite of the severe physical damage. Every moment passed like a day. We watched and listened, they were giving us little chance that she would survive or let alone awaken. Everyone was trying their best to keep us encouraged as we awaited the outcome. It was all in God's hands!

By Friday I was released from the hospital. I wanted to be in the comfort of my own home but it was not handicap accessible, so my son Jason and his wife Amber opened up their home. They brought in a hospital bed and I was taken by car to Lawrenceville, where they lived. It was bittersweet. I was so glad to be leaving the hospital, but Shelley had still not awakened, and the thought of leaving behind my precious wife was almost more than I could bear. In thirty years of marriage, we had rarely been apart from each other for long. Now, with her in the hospital, it appeared we could be separated for weeks.

I rested on Saturday. Now that I was out of the hospital, I seemed to be in more pain and my mobility was extremely limited. I was restricted, so I had to learn to use the transfer board to move from the bed into the wheelchair and from the wheelchair into the car. This board became my dear friend over the next eight weeks. The worst part, however, was feeling so helpless to intervene for Shelley. If only I could stand to my feet and look those doctors and nurses in the eyes and plead for the best care and intervention. But I was helpless to fight on my feet! My boys and family had to serve in that role.

On Saturday my boys and Dad went to the home in Conyers to install a wheelchair ramp from the garage into the house. I was ready to return home but I wanted to enter the home I left the

21

week before. But that ramp also spoke to me about the day Shelley would arrive back home. All the while I was thinking about my wife returning and walking in that door to greet Shelley with a kiss and a tall glass of cold iced tea.

By Sunday morning I was begging for someone to take me to the Atlanta Medical Center to see Shelley. We stayed in touch daily with the floor nurse of the Intensive Care unit but it was not the same as being there. Somehow you feel if you could be there something good would happen. So, on Sunday afternoon, Dad Berry helped me into the car with the aid of my transfer board. I was so fearful I would miss the transfer and land on my feet, or worse. I was the perfect patient, I had to follow the doctor's orders to stay off my feet because I had a battle before me and I wanted to stand to fight. I probably should not have gone, but my desire to see Shelley was greater.

I remember, as we pulled up in the front of the hospital, my heart was racing with anticipation. I couldn't wait to see her. I just knew that if I could say the right word or touch her skin she would awaken. Dad parked the car and I rolled on my own up the ramp into the front door. I entered the hospital anticipating a resurrection from her coma. It seemed like hours before Dad caught up to me and he helped me roll into the elevator. We arrived at the ICU and waited to be let in. I still felt so helpless! My heart was racing! I wanted to get out of the chair and run to her room. Finally, the intercom nurse said, "Mr. Berry you may come in". I rolled out in front of dad and pushed my way past the double doors into the intensive care room where Shelley was.

I wheeled up to the bed and looked up into her white ashen face. The machines were still roaring and pumping and she was still lying motionless, in a coma. Nothing had changed since having left the hospital a few days ago. I called for her nurse frantically hoping I could find some answers. I remembered they had great hope that within a few days she would be coming out of her coma.

I desperately needed someone to make it better for my precious Shelley and give me hope. Everything in me wanted to cry out, "Someone help me! Someone do something to help awaken my wife." With all the advancement of medical science there had to be someone who could solve this medical mystery Shelley was facing. Surely there was something they could do. Maybe they could operate on her brain or provide her some medicine to awaken her brain. Anything!!!

Finally, the nurse called in Shelley's surgeon, Dr. Henderson, to give us insight into her condition. Dr. Vernon Henderson was a kind, confident surgeon whose presence was calming. We immediately felt that Shelley was in wise and compassionate hands. He asked permission to do a tracheotomy on Shelley to make sure she had adequate access to oxygen. He explained that this 20 minute procedure would help alleviate discomfort and prepare her for awakening without constrictions. He also shared that "this morning her eyes opened". In spite of the positive news from the doctor, however, the tracheotomy still felt like a giant step backward, but we kept hoping for the best. We were so far over our head in trouble. The medical world is a strange place that has its own vocabulary and mysteries. You simply have to trust they know what they are doing and they are making the best choices.

Even though we felt out of control, we knew we belonged to God, and He was in control. God gave me a verse during this time that brought comfort; Jeremiah 30:17 "For I will restore health to you . . . says the Lord." We had confidence that God was going to bring Shelley through this crisis. Just like God parted the Red Sea, we believed that God was going to move the mountain before us and Shelley was going to return healthy, whole, and normal.

Over the next two weeks life sped by quickly. One of the big blessings came from our gracious friend, David, who stepped forward to provide me a car. It was one that I could maneuver with a wheelchair and handicap accessibility. This act of kindness was a reminder that God was sending people who would support us with prayers and compassion. We were not alone and God had not forsaken us!

After the first two weeks I sensed we were being prepared for the worst. This was not going to be a few weeks of coma and then rehab. The family was beginning an ordeal that none of us could imagine. Now, the doctors were telling us that although they believed she was going to awaken out of the coma that it might take longer than they first imagined – not welcome news! It could take many more weeks or several months.

The second Sunday after the accident I received a phone call from the neurosurgeon who had finally taken new scans of Shelley's brain. The conversation was solemn and disturbing. He shared in a solemn whisper that although her injury was small it was serious. He said, "If you could take a pen and place the tip in the area of her brain where it could do the most damage; it would be where Shelley's injuries are." I remember taking that phone call in the bathroom and slumping over in my wheelchair. I was numb and fear started to rise in my soul like nothing I had ever experienced. What did this mean long term? What could we do to solve this problem? There has to be a specialist or some treatment we can find! I felt overwhelmed. News like this is not processed well when you are fighting your own battles with your health.

That next week Dr. Henderson called the family together and informed us again the information that the neurosurgeon had shared Sunday. Things had not changed; there was significant damage to the thalamus portion of the brain. A blood clot had now formed in that area and other tests showed bleeding in other spots in the brain. Dr. Henderson said, "We are waiting on Shelley and when her brain is healed enough she will awaken". He also mentioned that though her injury was still small, the location of the damage made it critical. A spot the size of a pin head in that area could create incredible damage and there was no telling what the long term prognosis would be. My head was spinning!

During September Shelley battled with a lung infection that eventually turned into pneumonia, a collapsed lung, and a battery of tests. She also was given a stomach tube that would provide nourishment through an IV. Over the next few weeks she had many tests including more test on her brain activity. But all of these procedures were telling us that Shelley was being prepared for long-term illness. This wasn't going to turn around overnight. This wasn't going to be the type of miraculous recovery that you see in the movies. We were in reverse and not forward in this recovery! You might imagine the overwhelming fears, numbness, and unknowns we were now pondering.

During the month of September we actively waited. We waited on Shelley, doctors, tests, scans, prognosis, and more. Life seemed to be on hold for all of us as we waited for Shelley to awaken. We were given encouraging news that it could happen any day, but at the same time they were taking about moving her out of intensive care into a LTC center. The LTC is a place where they take patients who are either terminal or permanently incapacitated. We were told there was no way she would survive if we brought her home. Shelley would need care around the clock 24-7 care. And our Blue Cross and Shield coverage demanded we move her to a less expensive option. Now, the reality of our current and impending situation was starting to unfold before our eyes. We were in unchartered territory unimagined!

In addition to all of this, the hospital bills were accumulating. Even moving Shelley out of the Atlanta Medical Center was a hurdle. We visited several LTC centers and, after evaluating Shelley, most of them wanted cash as proof we could pay the bill. We are talking about "big cash" assurances. They had read her medical records and realized she could be there permanently and did not want to be responsible for her long-term care without assured payment. These were very troubling times for us! We felt helpless and sometimes hopeless!

We finally found an LTC center in south Atlanta called Regency Hospital. They had 24 hour care, ventilator support, respiration care, rehab options, and accepted whatever Blue Cross would pay for coverage at face value. The day they accepted Shelley, our whole family wept with joy. This was a tremendous answer to prayer after a long ordeal of indecision about where to take Shelley.

These times of crisis demand either fear or faith. I bounced daily from one to the other. I can hardly describe the polar feelings of those traumatic days. Here I was in a wheel chair, being cared for by parents in their late 70's. And at the same time having to make life and death decisions for my wife. Trying to put into words what life was like during those tumultuous weeks of September was a reminder of something that had happened in my past.

A few years ago I served on the board of Bethany Bible College as a trustee member. One of the most unpredictable and fearful parts of the flight was the jaunt from Bangor, Maine to St. John, New Brunswick, Canada. You never knew what unexpected delay or turbulence you might encounter in a small prop commuter plane.

I recall one trip in particular which was memorable for all the wrong reasons. During the flight the cabin lights went out. The air conditioner was shut down unexpectedly, and the temperatures on board begin to rise to unbearable degrees. We were engulfed in clouds and we could not see anything but darkness all around us. I remember thinking at the time, "this is it - we're going down". I remember praying with desperation like no other flight before or after. Across the intercom came the calming voice of the pilot, *"Ladies and Gentlemen fasten your seat belts and stay in your seat, we are experiencing a bit of turbulence but stay calm everything is under control"*.

Over the weeks of September we had numerous times when we felt numb, angry, guilty, hopeless, helpless, overwhelmed and in denial. Our emotions moved up and down constantly. The first few weeks all we could see were dark clouds and turbulence. We counted simply enduring each hour a victory. Then, after the first 48 hours, each day Shelley was stable was counted as a victory. Now we were facing an LTC center and endless weeks with no hope in sight of Shelley awakening.

The knowledge that there is a great Captain that has everything under control sustained us. I can testify that over the past fifty years I have seen God do marvelous things even under unbelievable circumstances. He has bailed me and my family out so many times it is plumb ridiculous. More than often, He has turned what seemed like a total mess into a miracle of His grace. I could not see God failing us at this stage of life. I know it might seem crazy and overly optimistic to a casual believer but I felt this unbelievable inflow of His peace. In spite of the chaos around me I fully believed my Captain had it all under control. During this ordeal I remember waiting expectantly each day to hear the voice of the Captain on the intercom say, *"Ladies and Gentlemen we are experiencing a bit of turbulence but stay calm everything is under control - please prepare for a landing."*

Each day therapists would come and start working with Shelley so her muscles would not atrophy. Daily we would receive the uplifting news, *"we still think Shelley is going to awaken, so be encouraged"*. One day several of the doctors pulled me aside and said, *"Make sure you bring Shelley back after she recovers so you can introduce her to me."* All wonderfully positive words, but we were desperate for more visible signs that she was coming out of the coma and would soon start rehab.

Each day as I visited the hospital in my wheelchair I would approach the drive praying this prayer, *"O Lord, please let me visit today and see Shelley awake, alert, and eyes wide open. Help me to see resurrection day!"* and each day I would leave devastated. I would spend three or four hours at a time with my bride praying for God to awaken her. I played Christian worship CD's and even compiled one with family and friendly voices. I put my cologne on her pillow. I placed her favorite candy bar, Butterfingers, in a small dish near her bedside and invited nurses to enjoy so the aroma might awaken her senses. Daily we talked to nurses about any sign of improvement. We pleaded with everyone to do all they could to help us! Many shared that they would stop by her room daily to whisper a word of prayer for her healing. Then I would leave, feeling I had visited a funeral. Oh, how life can change in just one moment.

In the book, Meeting God at a Dead End, Ron Mehl reflects on the Biblical Story of Joseph as he was waiting in captivity, wrongfully imprisoned for a crime he did not commit. Ron writes: "But for Joseph, time was moving in agonizing, painful slowness. Perhaps 10-15 years pass. That's a long time to spend in a waiting room. That's a long time to spend parked on a dead end. As it turned out, God was very much at work, right in the middle of the pain. God was working in the courts of Egypt. God was working in the weather patterns that circled the globe. God was working in his brothers' lives. And most importantly, God was working on Joseph's own heart, testing and probing and forming a young man who simply would not waver from his faith in God, even if life took him to the bottom of the dungeon, or the height of power and prosperity. But make no mistake about it. As God worked, the waiting was hard for Joseph ... bitterly hard."

Habakkuk 2 says, "*These things I plan won't happen right away. Slowly, steadily, surely, the time approaches when the vision will be fulfilled.*"

In my mind I often went back to the three weeks before the accident. I envisioned Shelley and me setting on the front porch with a big glass of cool iced tea in hand. We had just finished a hot August day of lawn work. I would see Shelley looking at me with those beautiful blue eyes and saying, "*Dan, don't you go and leave me!*"

That day I thought I knew what she meant. Looking back, I realize I did not have a clue! That pledge meant something even more significant than losing a few pounds and getting healthier. My heart, soul, and everything in me cried out, *"Shelley, I promise I will not leave you, no matter what!"* I was getting prepared to fight to the end if necessary. It was not an act of bravery but simply a pledge given at a wedding altar years ago. It was a pledge I meant with my whole being, and I was determined I would not break it.

CHAPTER TWO STUDY GUIDE:

1. Discussion: Have you ever experienced a crisis that caught you off guard? What were your feelings during that time? What did you learn about yourself and about God?
2. What sustained you during your times of trial or crisis?
3. Why do you think God sometimes chooses to allow us to go through pain and suffering for a greater good? Why?
4. In Genesis 39 we find the story of Joseph was one of being rejected by his brothers, sold into slavery, and tossed into prison for staying true to God in temptation. Read the story of Joseph in prison in that chapter and answer the question. How would you have felt in Joseph's shoes? What emotions would dominate your life?
5. Read Psalms 62:5-6. List everything you find about God's character in these verses that could sustain you during crisis.
6. Read Psalms 34:18. When have you felt close to God during a crisis or problem? When have you felt the furthest from God?
5. Is there someone you know of who is presently going through a crisis? Describe what they might need from their friends during this crisis? What do they need from the church? How could you be an encouragement to them this week?

Prayer:

"Father, I don't know what tomorrow holds. I realize that sometimes you lead us through difficult circumstances to teach us about yourself and reveal how utterly dependent we are on you. Keep me open to what you want to show me and teach me. Keep me from those hopeless feelings. Condition my heart to trust you more, even when I don't understand what You are doing. Use my difficulties and pain to make me more like You. In Jesus' name, Amen."

Chapter 3   I Believe We Can Make It!

Psalms 40: 1-2 "I waited patiently for the LORD; he turned to me and heard my cry. He lifted me out of the slimy pit, out of the mud and mire; he set my feet on a rock and gave me a firm place to stand."

"We must accept finite disappointment but never lose infinite hope."
Martin Luther King, Jr.

"Hope is the thing with feathers. That perches in the soul. And sings the tune without the words. And never stops at all." Emily Dickinson

I heard the humorous story of a priest, a minister and a guru who sat discussing the best positions for prayer, while a telephone repairman worked nearby listening intently to the discussion. "Kneeling is definitely the best way to pray," the priest said. "No," said the minister. "I get the best results standing with my hands outstretched to Heaven." "You're both wrong," the guru said. "The most effective prayer position is lying prostrate on the floor." The repairman could hardly contain himself. "Hey, fellas," he interrupted. "The best praying' I ever did was when I was hanging' upside down from a telephone pole."

The days that followed in the LTC center at Regency were days feeling like we were "hanging upside down from a telephone pole." We were praying hard but still feeling overwhelmed. When life thrust you in a crisis situation you are soon either crushed by it or you learn to survive. I believe there is a special gift of prayer when you are hanging upside down and feeling out of control. Problems come in all sizes, shapes and degrees of intensity. Much of life is not based upon the size of the problem but the decisions and attitudes we choose during the crisis.

Someone described it as "playing the cards you are dealt well". It has been said, "It is not what happens to you but what happens in you that matters." What we were facing as a family was

31

overwhelming. We could hardly make daily decisions, much less, could we see clearly God's purpose, plan, pattern, or a clear path out of our dilemma.

It seemed that for every step forward there were three steps backward. We tried to be as positive as possible as we shared the news with our friends. I am hesitant to confess this but, we had so many setbacks that we kept back the worst news for fear of losing or alarming our prayer partners. Inside the daily battle our faith was weakening and our choices narrowing. Humanly, it was looking more impossible every day. That's the way it felt when you are facing one defeat after another.

The stay at Regency Hospital started on another chapter in our journey. During this time we were pressed every week with seeing limited and insignificant progress. The tension of life and death was beyond the description of words. You could feel the compassion of the staff and their desire to see Shelley improve. They seemed to connect with our family; maybe it was the free Butterfinger bars, but I really believe they were pulling for us. But, when you looked into their eyes you could see their disappointment in Shelley's progress. It just wasn't moving ahead like everyone desired.

Pressure was coming from every side. Every physical problem Shelley dealt with was another setback and another battle with faith. More than once I cried out to God, "Where are you God? This is Shelley, your daughter who has served you." My nights lying alone in our big bed were filled with tears of grief and pain. First, there was pneumonia, then lungs collapsing, and staff infections. The list of the physical battles was so long it could numb the mind and break the spirit. It was a daily battle for Shelley's survival and that takes a physical toll on the whole family.

But the oasis of our journey was the fact that we were in a hospital that specifically dealt with acutely ill patients who need 24/7 care. Shelley was getting the best care that we could afford and probably as good as any hospital in the nation. But in the back of our mind we knew the clock was ticking. Eventually health insurance runs out or when significant progress does not happen they do not provide coverage. Eventually all patients either die or they are released to their family. Everything eventually changes and we knew that the changes in this journey seem to always be a higher mountain to climb and greater faith demanded.

There were small symbols that we used to daily remind us to take hope. Inside of the bag of belongings from the day of the accident was Shelley's pearl ring. Each of the two pearls on that ring represented a crisis of faith; one pearl for her battle with cancer and the second pearl was a reminder of her present battle in a coma. It constantly reminded me of the hope we had together in God. The ring became a symbol of my prayer for her awakening and her returning to her family. I purchased a gold chain and wore it around my neck to constantly remind me to pray and focus on healing.

That gold chain hanging around my neck was a promise reminder that one day soon I would place it back upon Shelley's finger. I would remind her of how faithful God has been to us through this trial. I anticipated by faith the day that I could look into her beautiful blue eyes and tell her of the thousands of people who prayed for her healing daily. With anticipation and hope we looked toward that celebration day!

During this time, I was struggling with my own rehabilitation. I was in a wheelchair as my bones were healing from the pelvic break. Each day I worked my rehab routine with a focus on healing and getting back on my feet. I felt driven to get better! Daily I would wheel myself from home to the car, from the car to the hospital, then back again. Never missing a day! Dad Berry was faithful in driving me to the hospital. For hours each day I would sit beside Shelley in my wheelchair and pray, sing, and talk to her as if she could hear me. I had heard stories of how some people in a coma later share how they heard the voice of loved ones even when they were unconscious. Perhaps this was true of Shelley, so we kept the faith and kept pressing for her awakening.

This also included visits from people and family. People from the churches in Georgia and Alabama came by from time to time to pray with Shelley. People anointed her, sang to her, laughed with her, told her stories, and reminded her of their love for her. There was no stone unturned to seek divine intervention. Everyone did anything possible to awaken her out of her sleep. Churches around the country prayed for her at least weekly. My whole life and prayer was myopically focused toward getting Shelley to awaken and return back to her family.

In times of desperation I understand why "faith healers" draw so many people. I remember thinking, "I am willing to try anything to awaken Shelley out of this coma". Yes, I was willing to pick her up and take her anyplace, anywhere, and to whomever. Someone suggested an oxygen chamber that had worked for other coma patients down in Florida. Others suggested natural cures and remedies. The suggestions were all well-meaning! When you are desperate you are willing to pursue any option to bring relief. But, Shelley was on her own timetable and we were all getting impatient.

Each day we visited the hospital hoping for a resurrection and we left disappointed and feeling like we had visited a funeral. Throughout these days the medical professionals assured us that four, five, or six weeks in a coma was not cause for alarm and that any day she could and should awaken. Of course the sooner she awoke the better long-term prognosis, and the longer she remained in the coma the more difficult the climb toward health and re-covery. One doctor mentioned that anything beyond the twelve weeks was statistically leaning toward a terminal situation. How we prayed "Lord, please let Shelley awake soon, please Lord!" Our time was in His hands!

No matter what type or quality of health insurance, it seems their number one focus is to get you out of the system. They want the bills to cease! From a pure financial perspective I can understand the need to watch the bottom line. But this was not just another statistic, this was my wife. After her condition did not improve immediately there was conversation with hospital personnel about the "what if's." We all had to consider the horrible fact that Shelley might be in a coma for the remainder of her life.

The doctors were telling us it was a waiting game. We were encouraged whenever we would see her fingers move or her tract motion with her eyes. Every small step whether real or imagined was a victory for us. But the insurance company was anxious. They knew that Shelley could be a long-term patient and in need of hospitalization for the remainder of her life. It seemed they were hedging their bets on the worst case scenario and the financial clock was ticking. They wanted to limit their liability and get her daily costs down significantly so decisions were coming. We could feel the pressure mounting!

Case managers weekly reminded me to be prepared to make some huge decisions unless Shelley started making faster progress. What I found out was there is weekly if not daily contact with the insurance company. Failure to make progress can result in a patient being released from the hospital prematurely. So not only were we fighting disappointment and anxiety with the slow progress of Shelley's physical recovery, we were battling impatient insurance companies and hospital pessimism.

After eight weeks of being in a wheelchair I went back to visit the doctor for the final x-ray's to assure the bone had healed on my pelvis. It seemed like an eternity before they called me to take the x-rays. They took the film then sent me back to the waiting room to receive the results. The doctor walked in with a big smile on his face and proclaimed, "Your x-ray's look good and you are ready to start walking again".

I was ecstatic! With assistance I rose from the wheelchair. For the first time in eight weeks I was standing on both feet, full weight bearing. Then the room started to spin! Then my mind immediately turned to Shelley. I had been off my feet for eight weeks and taking daily rehab. How would her coma affect her? The thought was overwhelming. How was she ever going to walk again, even if she came out of the coma today?

The next day, with the aid of a walker, I visited Shelley in the hospital that evening. It was a glorious day! I now could look the nurses and doctors in the eye. I felt like I could now fight even longer and stronger for her. It took me nearly a week before I begin to feel steady again on my feet, but this was a great personal victory! I could now champion the cause of my wife on my own two feet!

I will never forget the day I visited with Shelley around her seventh week at Regency. One of the head nurses pulled me aside to talk with me face to face. With an authoritarian tone of experience she said, "Shelley is a very sick lady. She may not awaken. Sometimes it is better if they die than linger for so long." Those words were devastating to my spirit. I was fighting so hard for my wife and striving to hang on to a positive attitude. It was as if this nurse had suddenly dumped cold water on my flickering ember of hope and confidence. Thankfully, her kind of encouragement was few and those words rare. I refused to accept her pessimistic view and told her very clearly, "I take exception. I love my wife and will fight for her until there is no more energy left in me or in Shelley to fight."

To this day, I think she was trying to help but her words were so discouraging. She was going by the facts and her medical experience. But, when it is your wife or your loved one fighting to stay alive, such objectivity and practicality often serve to devastate hope. For days following I battled with believing that Shelley would ever awaken from her coma. How powerful words can heal or hurt us in our faith and hope!

Proverbs 18:21 states that *"Death and life are in the power of the tongue..."* During crisis moments in our life, the words we receive and the words we speak are so important. Our words can encourage and be instruments of hope that bring light and inspiration in a time of need. If we are not careful though, what is intended to be honest words of practicality can actually tear down and steal the light of hope that may very well be the only thing that is keeping a person going. We never go wrong by choosing to speak life into others. I thank God for the hundreds of people who continued to keep our hopes alive by their prayers, kind words, and optimism.

After I completed my time in the wheelchair I returned back to work again. So each day I would go to work and then later in the afternoon I would drive to Regency to visit with Shelley. Each of these days started with a phone call to the head nurse to find out how Shelley rested during the night and if there was any progress made. Each morning I would ask the question, "Has there been any sign of Shelley coming out of the coma?" I always had a hard time leaving the hospital knowing that no one would be there with her for the next 24 hours but nurses and technicians. Oh, how I wished I had the strength and energy to spend every night with her!

One day the social worker pulled me into her office and notified me that Blue Cross and Blue Shield would no longer cover Shelley's stay at Regency. For a good long eight weeks we had been in Regency Hospital. It had become a comfortable oasis of compassionate and competent medical care. Shelley was still on oxygen, she had a stomach tube, was in a coma, and needed 24/7 care by trained nurses and tech's. I could not imagine taking her home, but the cost of her going to another long term unit was three thousand five hundred dollars a week and there was no insurance coverage for this type of care. We again were faced with the brutal reality of our changing situation.

So, after much prayer and counsel we decided to bring her home to Conyers. It was our only option! I did not know how we were going to care for her on a daily basis but we would try. I also remember feeling tired of driving those long miles each day to see Shelley. At least if she died it would be in a place she loved – her home. And we reasoned that if she died under our care at least she would be with her loving family. I did not have any medical or nurse training. And I confess I hate hospitals! I had never given a needle in my life. Truthfully, I did not know how in the world I was going to be able to rise to daily challenge of such a seriously ill patient. I was fully out of my expertise and comfort zone. I prayed, *"Lord, help me for I know not what I'm doing!"*

If there were ever two saints on this side of heaven it was my mom and dad. Dad and Mom Berry, in their late 70's, could have easily stayed home and prayed. Instead they placed their house up for sale in Salisbury, Maryland and decided to help me care for Shelley. They said, *"Dan you will never make it without help!"* Moving is never fun but especially not when you are in your late 70's. They made a life commitment to see us through this crisis. I don't know what I would have done without my mom and dad sacrificing so greatly. Mom said she would help me nurse Shelley every day and Dad committed that he would watch over her daily while I was working.

Though my boys were very busy they did what they could. A friend of our boys named Brad in Indianapolis felt led to provide financially so we could finish the upstairs of our home. Joshua, my son, was in Dental School in Indianapolis and he promised that he would come down to help as much as possible. In fact, Joshua even offered to drop out of Dental School to run to our rescue. I knew his mom would never want him to make that sacrifice and told him so.

The week after Thanksgiving was the day we had all dreaded. Our insurance company demanded Shelley be released to her family. So, we brought Shelley home. I will never forget that desperate Friday. This once proud and distinguished woman was tossed out like a bag of garbage. She was rolled into an ambulance with medical support.

I stood at the front door watching as the ambulance rolled up our driveway and the nurse and staff lowered her comatose body into a hospital bed in our guest bedroom. Her eyes were fixed in her head and looked upward to the ceiling. Her face had a pasty plastic look with no facial expressions. She was comatose! This was such a traumatic picture forever imprinted on my mind. I wonder if she recognized she was back home! We all felt so helpless to care for her daily needs and had no idea what to do. I've found, however, that when faced with overwhelming situations beyond one's gifting, perceived ability, or comfort, it's amazing what love will empower a person to do. We all loved Shelley and she needed us. So, together we rallied as best we could as a family to help her care for her ever need.

My job had allowed me the eight weeks needed during recovery, but now I was back to working full time. Several of our district leaders had stepped forward to help me out for the year including my friend and colleague, Dr. Dan Finch. Dan blessed me by carrying the yeoman's load during this time allowing me to focus on Shelley's health. Each day I would come home for lunch to care for her feeding, clean her, take care of her other personal needs, suction her phlegm, adjust her oxygen levels, and administer a host of medicines. I wanted to be as close to her as I could so at night I slept in the same room with her as she slept in a hospital bed.

Caring Bridge:
"It is easy to find yourself asking the question, "God if you are so loving and compassionate then why didn't you turn that green light at the top of the hill into a red light. Your probably more spiritual than me but I confess over the last three weeks I have asked my fair share of the "if's and's and buts" questions. I am comforted by the fact that the Bible is filled with some great saints who had pretty big questions for God. And thank God we serve a God that is big enough to take our most difficult and challenging questions without feeling threatened. During this time of crisis I have been overwhelmed by the evidence of God's compassion through His Church. Today Mr. Mike Hammond came by to install that restroom door, now making our restroom handicap accessible. Thanks Mike (and Priscilla),

Each night I would drift in and out of sleep watching over her every cough, breathing patterns, and needs. I remember waking up at least four to five times every night of life in those days to turn her body to keep from bed sores. Shelley had a breathing tube which meant I had to suction out her lungs many times, day and night, to keep her breathing easier. Sometimes there would be three or four times a night when I would have to get up and suction her lungs to keep her breathing.

I remember one night in those early weeks when Shelley was fighting for her very life. Her breathing was labored due to congestion in her lungs. I suctioned her tube probably four or five times that one night. I was all by myself in that room at 2 a.m. in the morning crying out to God for help. The next day on Caring Bridge someone wrote me and said that the previous night God awoke them at 2:00 a.m. and told them to pray for our family and especially Shelley. When I received that note it was like a life preserver to a drowning man. God heard my prayers! There is power in prayer. When we pray and when we listen to God's promptings for others.

My parents had moved in with me to help and I was very grateful. But I could see in their eyes that they were getting tired. I invited them after the first week of care at home to go visit my brother in Alabama. I would use the time to spend one-on-one time with Shelley. I knew I had to learn to care for her alone if God did not raise her out of her coma. They would only be gone for three days and I felt I could handle the duty and provide them escape.

How would I do caring for Shelley without relief? Something happened that weekend that became a turning point in her recovery. Within hours after they left, Shelley started to respond more than ever to my verbal commands. By the time the weekend was over and Monday came, Shelley was more and more responsive; eye tracking, movement, and awakening. There was no doubt about it, things were changing. We talked many times about the impact just being home must have had upon her conscious and subconscious mind. I believe to this day that even though she was in a coma she recognized she was home. At the end of the weekend Shelley was awaking more and more. We were seeing signs of hope!

Let me be clear, her awakening was not like the movies. It was not a beautifully dramatic scene where she suddenly opened her eyes, rolls out of bed, started talking and walking again. It was a gradual process of awakening. Every day, from that weekend on, she seemed to waken more and more. This was the first time in months that I felt we might just make it. Hope was being resurrected in our family. The encouraging thoughts of Shelley coming back to us were too good to believe. *"Thank you God, this is miraculous! We just might be able to make it!"*

Through this journey I've found that real life doesn't normally mimic the drama of the movies. It is much less immediate, less miraculous and more demanding. Shelley's brain injury was incredibly severe and she had been in a coma for 12 weeks. The woman that was now returning to us was not the same vigorous woman who lit up a room with her charismatic personality. It was a new Shelley—a Shelley who recognized us but could only slightly move her fingers or hands to signal. She used basic commands. She was significantly impaired and we were assured that she would never be the same. But, she was coming back to us. And who knows, doctors can be wrong!

Throughout Shelley's coma we gave her physical therapy to keep her body from atrophying. Each day we would move her legs and arms and do everything we could to keep her improving while she was unconscious. After her "awakening", her rehab moved to the next level quicker. We purchased weights for her to use to exercise her arms and start building muscles. She could not support her own weight at this stage, but over the next few months Shelley was able to sit up in a chair. She had to retrain her neck muscles to hold her head erect again. And occasionally we saw her begin to support herself. Walking was out of the question at this point of her recovery, but we took what we could get. Now, our house moved from hospital to rehab center.

Now that Shelley was showing progress the insurance company was ready to provide her physical rehabilitation. So, two times a week a specialist came into the house and worked with Shelley in building up her muscles in her hands, legs, and feet. Due to the long term coma her feet had started turning inward and there was a physical impossibility to walk without surgery. Those steps could be taken if we could get her into a rehab hospital and she kept making good progress.

We heard early in our journey about The Shepherd Center in downtown Atlanta. It was known as one of the best rehab places for acute brain injury in the world. When Shelley was in Regency Hospital we had tried to get her accepted but her condition and age was against her. She was flat rejected. Now, we reapplied and set a date for them to once again evaluate her for acceptance. They rarely took a patient from their home directly to the rehab center but we believed anything was possible. Our hope was that entrance into The Shepherd Center would provide the miraculous cure we had heard so many patients talk about. So, we worked and prayed and when we were finished we worked and prayed again. We were getting Shelley ready for her second and probably last chance for major rehab.

From experience I can tell you that when you've been knocked down and crippled, both physically and emotionally, standing is not an easy task. It is much easier to give up! It helps if you have a myriad of good friends who can walk with you, and talk you off the ledge. The very best friend you can have is yourself. You have to keep telling yourself often "you can make it." No one can do it for you. They can encourage you, support you, and cheer you on, but at the end of the day, the decision to stand firm in the midst of crisis and hardship is yours and yours alone.

Have you ever found yourself conversing with yourself? I have and I have done it quite often throughout my life. My office sits close to my secretary's office. Sometimes she will call out from the adjoining office, *"Were you talking to me?"* In embarrassment I respond, *"No, I was just talking out loud to myself again."* It is embarrassing to get caught talking to yourself but the truth is all of us do it. They say the danger is when you answer yourself. I've done that too!

Confession is good for the soul. Admit it! You have talked to yourself. You either consciously converse with yourself, and do it with gusto, or you unconsciously say things to yourself. Either way, the person that talks back to you is either a wonderful friend or a dastardly enemy, because what we say to ourselves will determine the choices we are making daily.

During this journey I found that I was preaching to myself in the guise of a prayer to God. I would say things like, *"God I know you are good"*, *"God, you have never failed me before and I know you are going to bring Shelley and me through this"*.

Everything I knew about God's character I reiterated continually to myself during this journey. There were also times, however, when I found myself quietly saying words that were destructive and faith bursting. Those discouraging times were capped by feelings that my prayers were not being answered, my situation was irreversible, and I was destined to fail.

In the Gospel of Mark there is a Jesus story that describes this trip. *"Let us cross over to the other side. And a great windstorm arose, and the waves beat into the boat, so that it was already filling. But He (Jesus) was in the stern, asleep on a pillow. And they awoke Him and said to Him, "Teacher, do You not care that we are perishing? Then He arose and rebuked the wind, and said to the sea, "Peace, be still! And the wind ceased and there was a great calm. But He said to them, "Why are you so fearful? How is it that you have no faith? And they...said to one another, "Who can this be, that even the wind and the sea obey Him!"* (Mk 4:35-41 NKJV).

Like the gospel story it seemed the first months of our ordeal was a picture of life out of control. There were the medical challenges, the persistent coma, and the daily stress of decisions beyond my wisdom. The winds were overwhelming and the waves that hit us were life shaking, but my confidence in God's character was what kept us all standing. I knew deep in my heart that God knew what He was doing and had a plan for all of this. I knew that in the midst of this turmoil, God's love for both Shelley and me was constant.

Mrs. Chas E. Cowman said, *"God does not test worthless souls! He loves much those whom He trusts with sorrow, and designs some precious soul enrichment which comes only through the channel of suffering. There are things which even God cannot do for us unless He allows us to suffer. Every wind that blows can only fill our sails."* I constantly reminded myself that Jesus was in the boat with me. We were not alone. God could be trusted.

When Martin Luther (Father of the Protestant Reformation) stood before his accusers and asked to recant his Protestant views of the Bible and God he made this memorable statement, *"Unless I am convinced by proofs from Scriptures or by plain and clear reasons and arguments, I can and will not retract, for it is neither safe nor wise to do anything against conscience. Here I stand. I can do no other. God help me. Amen."*

We were faced with having done everything that was humanly possible to do to help Shelley. The rest was up to God. This visual picture of Martin Luther came to my mind many times during this faith journey. As I've said before, sometimes just standing is victory. And there were many times during this journey when I heard the voice of Shelley speak those words said on the porch that summer afternoon, *"Dan, don't you go and leave me!"* The day I stood at that wedding altar and said, *"I do"* marked my life with commitment. I made a vow for *"better or for worst."* By God's grace I will keep it!

CHAPTER THREE STUDY GUIDE:

1. Discussion: Describe a time in your life when you felt like you were facing a dead-end experience in life? How did you respond emotional and spiritually?
2. Apostle Paul experienced some critical dead ends of life. Read 2 Corinthians 1:8-9. What role did faith play in Paul's crisis situation?
3. Read Proverbs 18:21. Think of a circumstance in your life when someone's words negatively affected your way of thinking. What could have been said to encourage you instead of defeat you?
4. What kind of spiritual conversations could you have with yourself to build your faith during times of difficulty?
5. What are some ways you can see the love of God demonstrated even in the midst of suffering?
6. Our crisis is not just about us getting through but how we use our pain to help others. How could you speak life into someone else's life this week?

PRAYER:

"Lord, help my faith to grow stronger in my daily experiences with problems, pain, and suffering. Help me to depend on you and not only on myself. Help me to know that "I can do all things through Christ which strengthens me". Lord, use me this week to speak words of encouragement and hope to the people I meet. Everybody I meet is having a difficult time in some way. So, make me a blessing by the kindness of my actions and the comfort of my words. In Jesus Name. Amen

When Faith Doesn't Make Sense

"Unfortunately, many young believers—and some older ones too—do not know that there will be times in every person's life when circumstances don't add up—when God doesn't appear to make sense. This aspect of the Christian faith is not well advertised. We tend to teach new Christians the portions of our theology that are attractive to a secular mind." – Dr. James Dobson

"Later Jesus appeared to the Eleven as they were eating; he rebuked them for their lack of faith and their stubborn refusal to believe those who had seen him after he had risen." Mark 16:14 NIV

"Faith consists in believing when it is beyond the power of reason to believe."
-Voltaire

As you review the last two chapters of our journey you will note that we have shared a path of deep discouragement and valleys of despair predicated by brief moments of joy. September 10th sent us propelling into a "red pill" experience that would not turn us loose. And, the journey hit us at all facets of our life.

There were not only the medical challenges but the financial expenses that begin to climb out of sight. Simply paying the deductible was a growing expense that had no end in sight. Thousands of dollars' worth of bills continued to accumulate daily. Over time I arrived at a place where I dreaded going to the mailbox to pick up the bundle of mail. It usually included four or five major bills that demanded payment immediately. Pressure was mounting!

The emergency air flight from the parking lot at Target cost close to $11,000. They would not accept Blue Cross and Shield as full payment. Eventually we settled that bill for over seven thousand dollars. In addition, every time we called an ambulance to take Shelley to the hospital, and this happened often, it cost us about four hundred dollars out-of-pocket. We had to find a way to solve this financial drain on our personal finances. If this was our "new normal" we had t0 find solutions and make adjustments!

God provided a loving family in a church at Wesley Chapel that provided his wife's handicap van on loan. We were able to travel back and forth to the hospital for tests, and scans without calling an ambulance. It might some small to you but this was a wonderful answer to prayer. I don't know what we would have done without such wonderful prayer partners, generous gifts and helpful friends. Seeing the advantage of a handicap van we eventually purchased a used one specifically for Shelley's transportation. This brought a little more independence to our family and gave us greater mobility.

Our God is a gracious God and often in the midst of trials and difficulties, I've found He has a sense of humor. One rainy day Shelley had to be taken to an area doctor's office a few miles from our house for a scan and x-rays. We loaded her in her wheelchair and used a borrowed metal ramp to push her wheelchair into the van. It was raining off and on throughout the day! Metal ramp! You get the picture! It worked fairly well getting her into the van. Then we drove to the doctor's office and pulled into the parking lot. Dad Berry and I were macho enough to be sure of our ability to maneuver Shelley in safety. We opened the van door and prepared to roll her down the ramp into the parking lot and office.

About the time the ramp was in place and we started rolling the wheel chair down the ramp the weather changed. Like on cue it started to down pour! Can you envision the picture of two grown men, one being 79 years old, fighting a wheel chair rolling out of control down a metal ramp in the rain? The wheelchair started to slip off the ramp and it appeared Shelley was going to fall to the pavement. "Oh, Lord, please help us, we can't let Shelley fall" was our desperate prayer. About that time two nurses, seeing our helpless plight, ran out of the office. They had been watching out the office window in horror. Then a Fed-Ex driver pulled into the parking lot and quickly hopped out of his vehicle to give us a hand. Once Shelley was safe we laughed about the helpless sight. What stories those people must have told their family that evening. But, that helpless feeling saturated us daily! We were living a desperate, day-to-day life!

Finally the clouds were lifting and we received a special phone call! We received the anticipated response from the admissions of The Shepherd Center in Atlanta. It was hopeful news! They had decided in favor of accepting Shelley into their traumatic brain rehab center. It seemed we were going to make significant progress in a specialized center. Within a few days we watched as an ambulance picked her up at the house and whisked her to The Shepherd Center. This was an awesome answer to prayer. We just knew if we could get her in the hands of this nationally acclaimed institution we would see significant progress. After all, they are known for their miracle stories of healing, cures, and recovery. Our hopes were soaring!

Within a few days Shelley was evaluated and they soon decided on surgery at the adjacent Piedmont Hospital to correct her twisted feet and ankles. This surgery would open up the possibility of her walking again. The surgery in simple terms was a small strategic surgical slice on the Achilles tendon to release those restricting muscles due to atrophy while in the coma. This in turn would relax the foot to its normal walking posture. After the surgery she would wear special boots for about four weeks until the feet and ankles healed in their correct walking position. Then she would start rehab by walking on parallel bars, cognitive therapy for the brain, and peddling a rehab machine. You might only imagine our excitement through each of these rehab advances. With great hope in our heart, we believed our Shelley was coming back to us. No, she would never be the bright, articulate, charismatic mother and wife of before but this was our new reality. It was a reality that we would learn to embrace.

During Shelley's time at The Shepherd Center I did my best to stay as many nights as possible with her in the private room. She would often ask, "Are you going to stay tonight?" She always had a smile and joy in her countenance when I could stay. She loved it when it was just us two together. So I made it part of my weekend date. We would enjoy a meal together, watch TV, talk, and welcome guests. I would talk with her throughout the night and often I would go to bed holding her hand just so she knew I was there. Eventually after about six weeks at The Shepherd Center she was released. We were thankful for all they did but we were still missing the miracle cure we were looking for. She came home better physically, taking steps with support, but emotionally it took her weeks to recover. In my heart I believe Shelley knew that her home was the safest and sweetest spot to be and so any time she left home it was an emotional reversal for her and guilt for me.

After The Shepherd Center release we arrived at a new discovery. You might say we moved from denial to acceptance. We realized at this stage of Shelley recovery she was emotionally drained from all the doctors, hospitals and cures. It was well over one year now on this journey! She wanted to stay home with her family. This is where she was at her best. As her family, we had to accept the reality that she was near the end of her recovery period. Emotionally she was at peace being with her family members who loved her and cared for her with deep love and overwhelming compassion. This realization was harder for me than the rest of the family. I would not accept that this was the best it was going to get. I constantly believed that there had to be a way or a chance to return Shelley to her previous health. Denial is such a beast to battle!

One of the downsides of her traumatic brain injury was the limitation of her speech. I asked her on several occasions what she was feeling and experiencing. She found it hard to describe without assistance. The best description of her condition was much like someone who had fallen down a deep dark well. She felt like she was constantly looking upward to the sunlight and where everyone else was living. She was living in one world and we were living in another. Shelley was not even slightly as verbal as she had been in the past. In fact, she had to be prodded to talk. Her thinking was skewed and clouded. Her ability to think clearly and articulate her feelings was limited to about a 4th grade level. But, at least I had my wife back! I was no longer alone! We had moved beyond the coma and we were making some progress. I would take any ad vances I could get and thank God for them daily. But these were not easy days either physically, emotionally, or spiritually!

During this part of the journey we went to doctors almost every week. If it wasn't a rehab appointment it was a doctor's appointment for some complication. The first year of her recovery involved getting her off of the feeding tube and eating again by mouth. This took numerous months and many daily regiments of rehab to prepare her to once again eat solid foots. The process was laborious and taxing!

Then, there was the long ordeal of getting her weaned off her breathing tube. For the first year Shelley had a difficult job of being weaned off of her tube and breathing naturally. Some people can be on a tube so long that they never again return to normal breathing. It took a specialist to slowly wean her off until eventually over a period of four months we saw positive results. I smile remembering the day we walked into the doctor's office and he removed the tube for the last time. She was breathing out of her mouth and not her neck! What a victory! I can still remember those days of small victories. One of the most memorable days was when Shelley was able to eat her first meal of mashed potatoes after almost a year being fed through a stomach tube. Each of these small victories we had to claw, climb, pray, and endure great hardships to see them become realities.

Going through a time of great loss and crisis can take a huge toll on your physical body as well as your faith. Daily we had thousands of Christians praying for Shelley to find total healing. We prayed for healing of her brain and healing of her body, yet our prayers for her full recovery seemed to go unanswered. It seemed inches beyond our reach. Our faith in God was strong. Our life was lived in step with the Word. It is difficult to understand when you have so many people praying and yet it seemed like there was so little change. A full independent living recovery seemed to always be steps beyond our grasp. Oh, how we prayed, worked, endured, and desired her return to full health!

We had friends, family and thousands of churches praying. I had people of great faith who had proclaimed that God had told them she would once again walk on her own and return to her former health. I had "assurance" from those who knew how to pray. They said that God had awoken them in the night and told them Shelley would be fully healed. I took comfort in their faith and confidence. But living with Shelley every day and hearing the reports from the doctors caused me some faith confusion. My faith wanted to believe the prayer warriors but we saw only small steps of recovery and most of the time they came after hard work and much pain. We clawed and scrapped for every inch of ground we carved for Shelley's recovery.

Often it takes time in the journey before you can see how much God is with you. His grace is sustaining you even when it appears imperceptible. Early in our journey we posted our story on CaringBridge. A local doctor heard about our family plight and he and his wife prayed about how they could help. He gave me a call one night about two weeks after Shelley had come home from Regency Hospital. He told me he was a Christian and wanted to help by providing his services as a doctor to visit in our home. He asked where we lived. I told him and there as a pause on the phone. We found out that he lived about three doors down in our same housing development. What an answer to prayer! These dramatic answers to prayer sustained our faith and gave us the "cups of cold water" to feed our hopes. We had experienced so many setbacks but God gave us those grace moments to remind us that we were not alone.

Every morning we had our normal daily regiment down pat. By the time a year had passed we were once again sleeping in the same bed. I would help Shelley out of the bed and into the shower, then help her brush her teeth, and help her into her favorite lazy boy rocker. As she progressed she was able to change into her own clothing as long as I laid them out for her. I would help her walk from the bedroom into the family room, with the aid of her roller walker, and help her set in her chair. I would go into the kitchen and fix her breakfast of juice, Boost, pancakes (with lots of syrup) and yogurt. While I showered and dressed she ate breakfast. I had to be very careful about her eating. The coma and her traumatic brain injury had left her with a less than adequate swallowing ability. If she ate something too large she could choke and if not watched could die.

One afternoon I happened to be home from work early. She was dealing with a stubborn pain. I gave her two of the large gel capsules of Advil. Within a few seconds I saw her start to turn blue. She could not breathe. The Advil capsule was too large for her too swallow. Suddenly, it was a life and death experience. I pulled her from the chair and into the floor and started CPR. Crying and shouting out for help! I did CPR for about 3 minutes while Shelley turned blue and then started turning black. I was desperate and exhausted and saw her dying before my eyes. I reached back in my decades old training of CPR when I lived in Allentown, PA. I tried to remember every maneuver taught to save her life. My mind was frantic for help! I was working and praying at the same time! I almost gave up and then I gave it one last time. Slowly it started to clear her throat. She cleared the capsule, swallowed and started turning a healthy pink about the time the police officer walked into the room. I was shaken and she was drained. She started breathing normally again. We almost lost Shelley that day! It also made it very frightening to ever leave her alone, even while she is eating. Her health was very fragile! And although my mom and dad stayed with her while I was away I knew they would never be able to provide the care and effort I gave her, it was just physically impossible. But it was a reminder of how thin a line we lived.

Now, let's get back to the daily routine. Once I was dressed I came back into the family room and helped her move to the living room. We had turned our house into a healing and rehab center. Dad Berry had used his carpenter skills to turn our living room into a place to rehab Shelley. We had a large eight foot table so Shelley could lie on the table and lift weights and exercise her legs and hands. We had a NuStep recumbent bike that Shelley would spend

20-30 minutes every morning. This exercise machine would develop stronger muscles by exercising her hands and feet. Dad Berry built parallel bars made out of four inch PVC pipe. The pipe was screwed to the wood floor and provided a great place for Shelley to begin walking on her own. And it worked! Soon Shelley was able to walk the ten foot distance on the parallel bars on her own. Our family was fully committed to helping Shelley get the best rehabilitation a family could give at home.

It wasn't long before Shelley was gaining strength in her legs and was walking with the aid of her walker. We had to be right beside her but she was making progress. I still remember the first time she was able to walk all the way across the parallel bar without assistance. There was a huge smile on her face that day! Each little event became a reason for us to rejoice and take hope that we could get her back to some semblance of health. Of course, we dared not leave her alone for any significant amount of time or she would fall. She needed 24/7 care by the whole family. It was "all hands on deck" for the Berry family.

The part of her brain damaged in the accident was the thalamus. The ramification of her damage was a lack of good judgment in dealing with risks. Whereas God has given all of us the ability to calculate the degree of difficulty or the degree of risk in taking an action, this was not working properly for Shelley. Shelley knew no healthy fear of taking a risk. What you or I would fear was of no risk in her thinking. She never calculated the danger of getting up alone, without assistance, to use her walker. The reality of what the consequences could be for her physically was not in her scope of thinking. This was so unlike the brilliant and calculating mind of the "old" Shelley we all knew.

Whenever we would take her to a new rehab center they would conduct an assessment of Shelley's health. They would ask the inevitable question, "So, how many times has she fallen and what list of damages does she have?" We always took great pride in telling them, to their disbelief, that she had not fallen and there were no new damages. We watched over her health like hawks.

54

I remember one eventful evening in particular. I had gone upstairs to the apartment on the second floor where my parents were living. Shelley was sitting downstairs in her lazy boy chair watching television in the family room. I was sitting on the couch and had only been there for about ten minutes. She must have heard our laughter and loud talking. Before we knew  it Shelley had taken the risky steps to crawl up the stairs without assistance and crawl on her hands and knees into the second story apartment. We were shocked and amazed. It was funny at the moment. And, Shelley had a mischievous smile on her face. However, if she was able to recognize her limitations and the risks of this action she would have never attempted the climb. We laughed and were proud she made it up safely but it was a wakeup call to be more vigilant in our care.

Shelley was making great progress. One night I came home and found her on her knees in front of the video cabinet. She had walked over to the cabinet with the aid of her walker and knelt down on her own. She was organizing the VHS and DVD videos in the cabinet all by herself. She was especially looking for videos of her family. We rejoiced in her actions and her progress but we privately shared our concern about her falling. She did not have a good sense of balance no matter how hard we worked at improving this weakness. This was part of the residual effects of the traumatic brain injury.

At this stage Shelley had moved out of the hospital bed in the guest room and into the queen size bed. I would still have to get up every night several times to care for her health. We used the guests bedroom because our friend Mike had helped us retro fit our bathroom for handicap accessibility. Her walker and wheelchair could easily fit in the bathroom. Dad Berry had also installed handicap bars around the bathroom to give Shelley extra support for maneuvering. We were committed to do everything in our power to keep her from falling and giving her some sense of "normal" in her life.

Every night Shelley would be put to bed about nine and I would take the time between nine and eleven to unwind and use for personal time. When you are the major caregiver you can burn out very easily. The steady stream of hospitals, doctors, and medications can emotionally and physically take its toll. With all the responsibilities I had little personal time. Even taking a shower was like taking a small mini vacation of solitude.

No matter when I would come to bed Shelley would always be wide awake and anticipating my arrival. She would turn her face toward me and say, *"Dan, I love you"*. I would look back and say to her, *"Shelley, I love you too."* These were her best moments of the day for both of us. Many nights I would ask questions to search her brain for any remembrances of her kids, our past and little stories. Her memory was best in the area of long-term memory stories. She may not remember what she had for breakfast but she remembered the stories of her past with a little help from me to jog those memories.

I personally struggled with the guilt of having been driving the car on the day of the accident. I have gone over in my mind thousands of times about the way I might have averted the disaster. Some nights I could not contained my guilt and my conversation would move to asking forgiveness. With tears running down my cheeks I would say, *"Shelley, I'm so sorry for the accident. Would you forgive me for what this has done to you?"* And Shelley every time would respond, *"Dan, it was an accident. There is nothing to forgive."* That was so much like the Shelley I knew. Shelley never had a callous or unforgiving bone in her body. She was always forgiving, loving and cared about people, her husband, and her family. Even in her disabled state she was extending grace and forgiveness like she had done for fifty plus years. Old habits are hard to break! As I think back to those days I believe God allowed those words of grace from Shelley to heal a little of my hurts and pains. I still struggle but perhaps God knew me so well that He knew I needed to hear those words of healing from the lips of Shelley.

The rehabilitation for Shelley was rigorous, demanding, and taxing for all of us. We took advantage of every available day of rehab that Blue Cross and Shield would cover annually. Many times it involved driving to a rehab center about ten miles away. It meant waiting for two hours while a speech or cognitive therapist would see her alone in an office. Sometimes it meant watching her struggle with her physical rehab knowing she was giving it every-thing she had and still coming up short. Shelley was limited even when we were so eager to see her make progress. Thinking back, perhaps my eagerness to help her return to good health and mobil-ity was driven further than her ability.

One night when I came into the bedroom she turned to-ward me with a smile on her face. She must have been lying there thinking of all the frustrations of rehab, tests, infections, set-backs, hospitals and trials. She turned toward me with a tear in her voice and asked, *"Dan, have I disappointed you?"* Those words struck my heart like an arrow from the enemy. This was not a question I had ever heard her ask. Somehow I felt I had sent an unintentional message to her that she was not trying hard enough. I broke under her question emotionally and replied, *"No, Shelley, you have never disappointment me. You have done everything you can and I'm so proud of you."* Her reply was *"Ok, good"*. And she turned and went to sleep at peace. She went back to sleep that night peaceful and rested well but I did not. I laid there most of the night, tossing and turning, and weeping. To think in her state of innocent disability that she would care about what I think. I beat myself up for days. To think of this broken woman, who was a shell of what she used to be, asking me if she had disappointed me. The truth was that I felt that I had disappointed her by not doing more.

These days were long, hard, and struggling days. My faith was tested. Anyone's faith is tested when you are watching someone you love face such a horrible condition. Her mind was limited, her physical was limited, and her emotions were forever changed.

I must confess that there were more than once when I cried out in my agony on behalf of Shelley. . . . *"Where are you God?"* And in those days all there came back to me was silence. Sometimes your pain is so loud that you cannot hear the grace of God. But there was one verse that grabbed my heart and my mind.

It is found in John 6:61-69

"Aware that his disciples were grumbling about this, Jesus said to them, 'Does this offend you? 62 What if you see the Son of Man ascend to where he was before! 63 The Spirit gives life; the flesh counts for nothing. The words I have spoken to you are spirit and they are life. 64 Yet there are some of you who do not believe.' For Jesus had known from the beginning which of them did not believe and who would betray him. 65 He went on to say, 'This is why I told you that no one can come to me unless the Father has enabled him.' 66 From this time many of his disciples turned back and no longer followed him. 67 'You do not want to leave too, do you?' Jesus asked the Twelve. 68 Simon Peter answered him, 'Lord, to whom shall we go? You have the words of eternal life. 69 We believe and know that you are the Holy One of God.'" NIV

There were times when I was very angry at God. There were times when God and I had some very harsh words. But here is the question all of us must eventually answer. Where do you go when you leave Jesus? I eventually had to confess that there was nowhere else to go when you leave God. If God choose not to give us our miracle would I leave my faith? Would I pursue another god or another answer in the medical field? Truthfully, all I had at this stage of my battle was God. So the words of Peter were powerful to my soul during this stage, *"Lord, to whom shall we go?"* The response I eventually wrestled over the months was. . . *"nowhere else"*.

It seemed that all that we had done for Shelley did not matter much. We had gone to the best hospitals. We had sought out the best neurological doctors. We had taken all the experimental medicines. She had spent over a month in The Shepherd Center rehab unit with some of the best professionals in the world. And at each of those steps toward her recovery I spent days with doctors and nights on a hospital cot. I was willing to go to any extreme, pay any amount of money, to reclaim my wife and the mother of my children back to her former self. But, with the best we could do it appeared that Shelley would never return to the person we all knew and cherished.

Many nights after putting her to bed, I sat in my chair and wept and cried out to God. My faith in God was being tested like never before in my life. Here was my precious wife that I deeply loved, so helpless and totally unaware of what was going on. Soul searching questions swarmed in my mind like honey bees around a hive. Why would God not create a miracle of healing for my wife? I had seen Him do it for others. Would not a miracle bring Him greater glory? Would not a miracle of Shelley's healing cause the unbelievers to fall down and worship Him as mighty God and healer? I was dealing with what the theologians call, *"the dark night of the soul"*.

And during those times I bargained with God. *"God, please take me in exchange for Shelley's return to heal"*. I understand how people can take drastic actions to seek alternative cures and healers. I was willing to sacrifice anything and everything if only God would bring my wife back to me. But no amount of prayer, professional help, medicine, rehab, or bargaining brought relief to Shelley or me.

There were moments in which I considered tossing in the towel of faith. But John 6 played like a movie in my memory. *"Lord, to whom shall we go? You have the words of eternal life."* I had tried everything that humans could do. When you leave Jesus where else do you go? I knew all I had was faith in God.

On December 4th, 2007 I wrote in the Caring Bridge journal:
"As I look back over the last 12 weeks (since the accident on September 10th) nothing seems to make sense. I could name a thousand different trials that would better fit who I am and who Shelley is much better. The trials I could conceive would have better fit my personality as well as Shelley's. Beside the actual brain injury that Shelley sustained, this "wrong size" facet is the most difficult to adjust. Truthfully, I can handle Shelley's death (I know she is bound for heaven and we'll spend eternity together). I can handle her miracle healing and a life lived proclaiming God's glory of healing. There are so many scenarios I could have chosen for myself, but God doesn't permit me to choose. . . . I am simply asked to trust. I am asked to trust Him when He doesn't make sense or even when He seems unkind or ungracious."

But "simply trusting" is not an easy task. If you've ever had to do it you know it can be incredibly difficult. It requires letting go of what you want and surrendering it without control. It means resting on that which you cannot see. It involves admitting that you are beyond helpless in the situation and at the mercy of the One who is greater than you are; the One who doesn't always act or work like we would desire. It means coming to the realization that God's plan for your life may be vastly different from the one you have chosen or written mentally in your mind. It means releasing the dreams you had for your future to God.

Do you know what it's like to make plans for your life and then have those plans and directions changed? A big part of this Christian walk is learning to trust God even when His purposes and plans look absolutely impossible. As I look back over my life, so many of the decisions Shelley and I thought were headed a certain direction were altered by God's better plan. There have been so many opportunities I thought were going to materialize and so many decisions I was planning to make . . .but God had another plan.

God has the right to change our plans. He is, after all, God. Because He is in control He has the final word. This is where the need to trust comes in. It's a lesson I'm working at every day! I have not arrived, I still feel like a kindergarten student in the school of faith.

Since the day of the accident, if it had been up to me, I would have written the script much differently. In my wisdom I saw no need to make this drama of Shelley's coma last so long. I saw no need to have her rehabilitation so limiting. I saw no need to be tested with small victories and then big defeats. But I realized I wasn't God. I didn't have the final say. So I waited upon God's purpose to prevail. Perhaps He would still heal her.

One time I humorously commented to one of my pastoral friends that over the past weeks I had considered, reconsidering the Catholic doctrine of purgatory. The experience of being "between heaven and hell" was one of the best descriptions of my daily life at that time. Hold tight you doctrinal purist, I said "humorously".

Living the "in between" place in life is not an easy place to make your home. Some call it the "muddle in the middle". Again, it is a matter of simply trusting, waiting, and believing. All three of which I confess I am not a stellar student.

I was reading through the "guestbook" on the Caring Bridge site one day and was struck by a particular post about Louie Giglio's message entitled "The Megaphone of Hope." Louie spoke about a greater purpose in life; it is a deeper reality to live in. He said that our goal is to glorify God whenever light shines on us. Light can shine on us for a variety of reasons.
One time in which light shines on a person particularly bright is during tragedy and that during those times our job is to shine that light back on Jesus. Louie also talked about how suffering hands give us a megaphone to broadcast the message of the goodness and greatness of Jesus as loud as we can and people that hear you will be forever changed.

Suffering is our servant. We are not its servant. Suffering amplifies the core of what we believe; it's the megaphone that broadcasts our life's message louder. When one person stands on the doorstep of tragedy and speaks of the faithfulness of God, people's lives are turned around.

During this time in my life, my prayer for our family was to stand in the face of tragedy, shout through our megaphone of pain and suffering and declare loudly to the world that God is still good. I realized that this may be the loudest our family will ever be heard. This tragedy has actually given us a stage to broadcast the fact that God is faithful!

Much of life is beyond our ability to control. In an instant our life can change forever! We cannot prevent tragedy and no one is ever so blessed of God that they are exempt from pain and hardship. We do have a choice though. We can choose to make suffering our servant or we can choose to take it captive and use it for God's glory!

Throughout this whole process I found myself praying as Job did when his life began to crumble at his feet.

Job 1: 20-22 "Job got up and tore his robe and shaved his head. Then he fell to the ground in worship and said: 'Naked I came from my mother's womb, and naked I will depart. [c] The LORD gave and the LORD has taken away; may the name of the LORD be praised.'"

One of the toughest battles of faith is realizing that God does not have to give an explanation for His actions. He owes us nothing. The fact is that true faith does not hinge on understanding the reason for what God does; rather it rests on trusting even when His actions make no sense and the explanations evade our comprehension. Sometimes the only answer God gives you to stand on is, "Trust me. I know what I'm doing." That was the answer He gave me and that was the answer I had to stand on.

I wish I could say I stood firmly on it all the time. That would be inaccurate. I wobbled while standing on it. I stepped off it some days and then by night fall had stepped back on it! But I stood! Weakly, feebly, humanly I stood!
And sometimes simply "standing" is victory!

CHAPTER 4: Study Questions:

1.Discussion: What do you think the author means by the statement, "Sometimes simply 'standing' is victory?" Describe a time in your faith journey where God appeared to make no sense? How was your faith challenged during this time? How did you make it through this challenge with your faith intact?

2. Read John 6:61-69. What lessons on trusting God do you see from this passage?

3. What did you learn about God during that crisis of faith time? What did you learn about yourself? What were the thoughts that brought you peace?

4. What does Proverbs 12:5-6 say about trusting God to you?

5. Read Job 1: 20-22, what does it mean for you to praise God in your trouble?

6. Perhaps you know of someone going through a similar trial of faith. What would you declare to them about trusting God through your "Megaphone" of life experience and suffering?

PRAYER:

"Lord, I struggle to trust you when it is so difficult to see your hand in my life. The journey I am going through doesn't make sense right now. I have faith I just need help with those areas in my life that stretch my faith. I know there is no where else I can turn too but you. Lord, I'm not asking that you take me out of the storm but I am asking that you give me peace in the storm."

Chapter 5 Adjusting to the New Normal and Beyond

"Our tendency in the midst of suffering is to turn on God. To get angry and bitter and shake our fist at the sky and say, "God, you don't know what it's like! You don't understand! You have no idea what I'm going through. You don't have a clue how much this hurts." The cross is God's way of taking away all of our accusations, excuses, and arguments. The cross is God taking on flesh and blood and saying, "Me too." — Rob Bell

"My grace is sufficient for you, for my power is made perfect in weakness." Therefore I will boast all the more gladly about my weaknesses, so that Christ's power may rest on me. That is why, for Christ's sake, I delight in weaknesses, in insults, in hardships, in persecutions, in difficulties. For when I am weak, then I am strong." 2 Corinthians 12:7

"For every problem there is a promise and for every promise there is a provision." – A faith reminder note placed by Shelley on the kitchen cupboard as she started her 8 weeks of radiation.

We were making good progress about a year and a half into this journey. Shelley traveled with me in that conversion van almost every Sunday. Mom and Dad would ride along and help out as needed. Life had changed drastically but we were adjusting to our "new normal". I am amazed at the ability of the human soul. What we would never accept in one moment we can adjust too gradually over time. God was helping us to adjust and see possibilities that we could continue our life and ministry. It would be different but we could do it together.

My sons would come home from time to time to help out around the house. I especially appreciate my son Joshua and his wife Misti. Joshua was still in Dental School and Misti was working at a dental office. They would leave Indianapolis, and travel eight hours for the weekend. When he arrived he would say, *"Dad, I'm here to help out and give you a break. What do you want me to do?"* The whole weekend was not about him relaxing but about helping out around the house. I am so thankful for the times they came to visit their mom and help us around the house.

As we moved into the second year we did our best to make peace with Shelley's handicaps. On two different occasions we took her on a cruise to the Gulf of Mexico and the Caribbean. Debbie Berry, my brother's wife, was a wizard at finding discounts on five day cruises. I did not know how long we had together so there was never an expense spared.  I attempted to make her life as comfortable and as near to normal as possible. Every trip would tire her out but we could see the smile on her face and the joy in her heart because she was with us, her family. If you saw us in those days you might have taken pity on us but we had joy in spite of our trials. We were together as a family— Dad Berry, Mom Berry, Shelley and me. That was what mattered— family. We were not facing this crisis alone!

Even when you are dealing with a crisis, life moves on for everyone around you. And sometimes there is crisis within the crisis. Shelley's mom and sister, who lived in Croswell, Michigan, visited us several times to see Shelley. But now Pauline was facing her own health crisis. Pauline, Shelley's mom, was diagnosed with cancer and by the time the doctors had found out the extent of her illness it was too far along to be treated successfully. The doctors tried to provide treatment but the cancer was aggressive and she was given months to live. Within a few months she had moved in with Pat and Susan Green, her daughter. They cared for her every need. But it wasn't long before the dreaded call came, *"Mom has passed away."* Within a day we were packing and getting ready to head to Michigan for the funeral. We were ready to leave when the transmission went out in the handicap van. We took it to the local Amoco transmission shop and after the diagnosis found it would take another week to repair. So, we had to rent a van and off we drove in the dead of the winter to Michigan for the funeral. One time we even had to dig the van out of a snow bank due to the heavy downfall. It took us about two days to arrive in the area and two days for the viewing and funeral. The pain of this event was to know how much Shelley would have meant to her sister and mother if only she was back to health. All she could do was cry and look on as others helped out. Each trip we took was a good time for Shelley but it took a toll on her health and energy.

One Saturday morning, within a few months of Pauline's home going, I received a phone call from my cousin in Delmar, Maryland. She said, *"Dan, did you hear that your house burned down last night?"* A few years ago I had purchased a very small inexpensive home to use for a possible retirement home. When asbestos shingles were discovered on the home it forced me to either remove them at a huge expense or sell. I chose to sell to the renter and I held the mortgage on the property. A few months before he had missed several mortgage payments. I also discovered he had lapsed in his  property, fire, and casualty insurance. So, I paid the yearly insurance payment for him. Thankfully, I was now breathing a sigh of relief. I thank God for those missed payments that flagged the insurance man to call me. At the time they looked like a problem but looking back they were a blessing. For the next year, I was serving as the trustee on the rebuilding of his home. Life knows no relief in times of crisis.

One weekend we traveled to the furthest western area of our ministry territory in Jackson, Mississippi. The weekend went off without a hitch. Shelley, mom, dad and I traveled about eight hours from Atlanta in the conversion van. Shelley refused to lay down on the coach in the backseat but always felt more comfortable in the big captain chair. She wanted to sit in her usual spot, right beside her husband. She felt at peace in that van as much as any place; well any place besides being at home in her lazy boy chair.

That weekend Shelley seemed to be making more leaps of progress. She appeared more awakened, alive, and mobile. You could see it in her face. Her confidence was coming back. She would never again be the same woman but she was still improving. It was late Sunday afternoon when we left for the eight hour trip home. We arrived about ten o'clock Sunday evening and emptied out the van. I got Shelley settled into bed and as quickly as possible collapsed into bed myself. I slept all night soundly and hardly remember anything until morning.

I was awakened about seven o'clock in the morning with Shelley beside my bed. She had gotten out of bed with her walker, on her own, in the early morning hours unbeknownst to me. I asked, *"Shelley what are you doing out of bed?"* This was the first time I had ever known her to get up early without assistance. She said, *"I went to start a load of laundry and I fell."* This would have been the "normal" Shelley before her brain injury, but not anything I had known in over a year and a half. My mind raced back over what she said again. Then she said the words I had never wanted to hear, *"Dan, I fell."* Those words crashed into my mind like a bomb exploding. Later that morning I asked her to show me where she fell. The nearest we could understand was that she fell in the dining room on the way to the laundry room pushing her walker. Perhaps she fell on her hip against the dining room table. To this day we still are baffled by how she pulled herself out of bed without detection and took the initiative on her own to wash clothes.

I asked, *"Did you hurt yourself Shelley when you fell?"* She said no at the moment but I knew time would tell. As the day progressed we only prayed that there were no broken bones. She started to walk with the aid of her walker but with great pain in her face. We could only pray it was a bruised hip or leg. Two days went by without seeing a doctor or going to the emergency ward. We placed ice on the hip area regularly. Finally, after the evening of the second day I took her into the emergency room of Rockdale Medical Center for observations and a revealing x-ray. I was hoping, praying, and believing that this would only be a bruise that would eventually heal.

I can still see the doctor walk back into the cubical with the x-ray in hand. She said, *"Shelley has broken the socket in her hip and will need a hip replacement."* My countenance dropped and my heart began to race. Those words were the last words I was ready to hear. This was not the news I was expecting. She was making such good progress mentally and physically how could this happen? We had adjusted so well to our "new normal." My immediate cry out to God was, *"Why God? Why Shelley and why now when she was making such good progress?"* *"Lord, she has gone through so much over these past months and years why this?"* I was broken hearted for Shelley and for our family.

Within a few hours the paperwork was completed and Shelley was admitted into the hospital. I cried out in exasperation, *"Here we go again God!"* with a sense of denial. We were beginning another chapter on this difficult journey. Someone has referred to these events as "life body slams." It was surely that and more that evening. There was a numb feeling running all through my body. I knew this was not life threatening, but another surgery could be devastating for Shelley's mental and physical rehabilitation. Could we all endure more trials, travels, and long nights in the hospital? I did not know, but I was about to find out.

When you are caring for someone over such a long period of time it begins to harden you to reality. When news like this comes it leaves you with a sense of apathy and physical numbness. Your emotions have learned to go into apathetic neutral. You begin to protect your heart from the pain of disappointment. You become callous to save yourself from that internal devastation. You soon learn to move through the stages of grief quickly and accept the reality of your situation while praying for miracles. If you are not careful you can lose hope quickly and become bitter and cynical. This was a daily battle in those days. And I believe it is a daily battle for those dealing with long-term illness where they face one battle after another without relief. Ever so imperceptible you start to lose hope and become callous to bad news and the next trauma.

All through my life I have had great faith in our medical system: doctors, nurses, and technology. I've seen elderly people fall and break a hip and continue to live a productive and mobile life. But Shelley was fighting more than the physical challenge of a broken hip, she was fighting the acute traumatic brain injury. Shelley was not the same person as when she faced her battle with breast cancer. Her brain injury had left her less than sharp and mentally incapable to fight this battle. I was all alone in the decision making process. Shelley depended on me to be her protector and make the right call. There was the pressure of being alone facing every enormous crisis decision. So, once again we were facing an uphill battle with no end in sight.

Within a day the surgeon had operated on her hip and re-placed the old hip unit with a new ball and socket. The surgeon said that the surgery went well. Due to her complicated breathing after the auto accident I'm sure she was not an easy patient. Little did we know that this hip surgery would not be the ending of a problem but the beginning of more problems and new challenges.

When I walked into the recovery room to see her she was doing well. They soon had her trying to use the walker in her hospital room and walking down the hallway with the aid of her walker. But I could see the grimace in her face due to the pain in her hip. I thought to myself that it would take time for the tissue and muscles to grow around the new hip unit. Over time the doctors had said the pain would subside and her mobility would increase.

Over the next few months we did our best to provide the rehab necessary for Shelley to get back to the level she had been before the fall. However, the whole family noticed something else had been lost in this crisis episode; her mental faculty was not the same. It did not seem her mind was as sharp and her optimism seemed to vanish. She was not the Shelley of the weekend before her fall. As I look back to the falling accident I can see it could have devastated her self-confidence and her long-term hope for recovery. Though

Shelley was not the same person due to her brain injury, she was there deep down inside. This latest surgery was an emotional reality check for the Shelley down deep inside. Could she be giving up? After a few months of rehab Shelley was noticeably less mobile. She was in utter pain in her hip most of the days. The surgeon said, "She'll recover, it just takes longer for some people than others." I did not think that her recovery was making progress at the pace promised and the pain in her face made her days miserable. I continued to see her orthopedic surgeon, but his advice and prognosis of "just wait" was not satisfactory for me. As a caring husband, I had to fix her pain and help her get back to where she was before the fall.

Finally, I received a referral from Rev. Hugh Pope for a doctor in Lawrenceville, Georgia that had helped him and his wife. We made an appointment and went to see this specialist as soon as we could. He was everything Hugh had promised—kind, wise, insightful, and capable. He seemed to be committed to finding out what was wrong. He did not push us off by saying, *"let's just wait and see."* Instead he said he would get to the bottom of what was causing the severe pain and help us resolve it. Thank God for this precious doctor who was willing to help us find a solution to her enormous pain. He was willing to look beyond her mental capacity and find a solution. There was a sense of relief knowing we might actually get to the end of this problem.

After several more x-rays and scans his diagnosis revealed that there was slippage on the metal hip replacement in her leg. The surgeon at the hospital had placed a smaller unit in the hole and it was moving and the friction was causing Shelley pain. Can you imagine the pain Shelley must have been bearing all these months of rehab? I felt so guilty for pushing her in days of exercise now knowing that hip unit was rubbing against bone. His recommendation was a medication that would cause the bone to grow around the metal hip implant. It was the first stage of treatment and if it worked there would be no need for corrective surgery. What a relief! Maybe we could see progress once again!

71

So, we begin this new regiment of medication. Within a few weeks we could see an improved difference in her countenance. Shelley did not seem to grimace in pain and her mobility was starting to improve. I started to once again breathe a prayer of hope.

We just might be able to pull out of this crisis and enter back into our "new normal!" But, her emotional and mental advancements were not at the same level as those pre-fall days. Not only was she not as mobile, but she was also less hopeful and cheery as before. Something had changed since her hip transplant and the whole family noticed. We could only hope that with a little more time at home she would regain the mental and emotional health she had lost during the hip surgery.

If you have not caught the rhythm of this journey by now let me explain. Over the past two years it has been an up and down journey. We would make progress but at a much slower pace than we would have ever imagined. And just about the time it seemed we were settling into a "new normal" something would change drastically. We usually visited a hospital or doctor monthly and sometimes many times a month. Sometimes it was an infection, other times lung congestion. It took almost a full year from the time of the accident to get her weaned off of her breathing tube. It took her almost nine months to get her back eating by mouth. We even went to an orthodontist to help correct and straighten her teeth that had been shifted in the accident so she could chew again. But, it seemed that every small victory was followed by a slide backward. I will tell you that over a period of time the hard fought battles take a toll on a caregiver's health as well as the emotions of the one being cared for. I was stressed and Shelley was weary. When some people get stressed they stop eating – I start! That lifestyle takes a toll on your health both physically, mentally, and spiritually.

I was born in Virginia but raised on the Delmarva Peninsula of the Eastern Shore. During much of my upbringing our family lived about five miles from Ocean City, Maryland. Most of my early childhood experiences revolved around the water—fishing, clamming and crabbing. I have always enjoyed both sports because of their culinary delight. Crabbing is one fun sport and cream of crab soup afterward is the delight of the Chesapeake area.

To go Chesapeake Bay blue crabbing you need a line, bait, and a sturdy bushel basket. The basket is for the crabs once they are caught. When I was a teen, it is normal to catch many dozens in a few short hours of fishing.

Rarely do you have to worry about keeping crabs from crawling out of the bucket. Crabs have an uncanny and selfish tendency to hold on to each other. If one energetic crab tries to crawl out of the basket, another selfish crab will pull him back in. It is such a sight to see and a picture of life many times. They say "misery loves company" and the crabs must agree.

In a real sense Shelley had tried to crawl out of her handicap and brain injury. Whenever she made progress to climb out she was pulled backward just like those crabs in the basket. I want you to catch a little flavor of what Shelley was enduring daily. Shelley had been restricted to the "basket." Can you imagine the "pull" on your soul, weariness of spirit and the atrophy of the body? This is the "pull" that Shelley dealt with every day of life. And of course, every physical set back was another pull backward into the bucket for all of us.

The reality of Shelley's condition and our situation in life began to settle in over a few years. We realized that she would probably never rise any higher than she was the day before her broken hip. Something had happened within the soul and mind of Shelley after that day. Maybe she knew it as well. I can only imagine what must have crossed her mind the months after surgery. It just seemed like she was giving up! And "giving up" was not in Shelley's spirit. She was always the one who saw some positive in every dark cloud. She was born with a "silver lining" personality. She was the eternal optimist who always believed good days were coming after the bad. Now, she was giving up! And I was fighting the same pull!

Each day during these two years I would go to work at the office. I diligently kept my appointments and visited the places that needed a visit. But I will assure you that my heart was always back with Shelley. It was nothing to call back several times an hour just to check with Mom and Dad Berry about Shelley's progress. And I was always worried about her falling, chocking or having a turn for the worse physically.

One Tuesday morning I received a call from Mom Berry. She said something like this, *"Dan, Shelley is sweating and in pain. Something is not right I think you need to come home."* I promptly left the office and drove those two miles as quickly as I could. As I drove home that morning I was praying, *"Oh, God what is it this time! I don't have the energy or the strength, please help me God!"* I arrived home to find Shelley in the bathroom sweating profusely and struggling physically. It was nothing like I had seen up until this time. Something was happening physically and I knew it was serious and she needed immediate attention.

I grabbed her and placed her seated in her walker. I took her in the car to the closest hospital. Before the accident Shelley and I talked about what hospital we wanted to use. Everyone has their choices as you play out those imaginary scenarios. Hers was, *"Dan never take me to . . ."* Those remarks came to my mind as I was rushing her back to the emergency center of the hospital she did not want to go. It was the closest hospital to the house and time was of essence. I had no choice but it was one of those crazy thoughts that flooded my mind that day on the three mile journey to the hospital.

Once we arrived they ushered her into the emergency ward and begin to diagnosis her problem by running tests. Up to this point I was always very aware of her physical problems. I would go with Shelley to the doctors and share her medical history and serve as a translator between Shelley and the medical personnel. Most of the time I had good insight to share with the doctors that helped them in the treatment. Our family doctor even went as far as to

74

say, "*Dan you probably know more about the health of Shelley than anybody in her life.*" But this was something out of the blue that I did not see coming. I could not help the doctors at the emergency room. I did not have a clue what was causing her symptoms.

The first blood test came back to reveal that it was an infection. Over the last month one of those nasty infections had raised its ugly head again. She was already being treated with medication but it was back. It was back again with a brutal vengeance. Being in the hospital so long, Shelley had caught a staph infection that was not treatable by normal antibiotic medication. It usually took a heavy dosage of antibiotics and several cocktail antibiotics working in tandem to bring relief. That would at least explain her sweating and her deteriorating physical condition.

She was placed immediately into a room for further diagnosis and treatment for her infection. I stayed overnight several evenings with her. She seemed to be getting better but slowly. Her blood count was improving and the sign of the infection was dissipating. Everything seemed to be moving in the right direction until one lunch meal. I was feeding her and she vomited out a black bile. She started to chock on her own vomit. Something was more serious than originally diagnosed.

We later found out that along with her infection she had a bowel blockage. This could have been caused by the medication, infection, or a host of other reasons. With the bowel blockage she was not able to fully take advantage of the natural method to expel the infection from your body. There was no outlet for those toxic waste products to leave her system. She was being poisoned! The blockage in essence was working against her healing and recovery.

They rushed her to the emergency ward and started her on stronger medication but still no release of the bowel blockage. Eventually they tried to have her swallow a white liquid substance so they could get some pictures of her blockage. She was so weak and sick she could not keep it down and every time she vomited the white liquid she started aspirating. It seemed we were fighting a losing battle and time was of the essence.

She had now been in the hospital over a week. The days were moving by so slowly. Every day it seemed we felt more helpless and out of touch with Shelley's doctors and staff. One day it seemed she was improving and another day she was taking steps backward. No one seemed to want to sit down with us and talk in depth. We would grab a doctor whenever we could but the response was always, "we'll see."

On the same morning the nurse came in to give Shelley that white liquid for her bowel obstruction test, one of the doctors walked into the room. She asked if she could sit down and talk to us in private. My heart started to race! She walked down the hallway around the corner to a bench seat. My son Jason was sitting on my left and the doctor was facing both of us. She looked me in the eye and said, *"Dan, we've done all we can do. Shelley cannot keep down the test medicine so we can't operate without knowing where to operate. We are arranging for her to go into hospice."*

I heard the word "hospice" but it seemed to go right over my head. What she was saying to me

Caring Bridge- Feb 28: Shelley is now home and is resting comfortably. We have once again turned the bedroom into a very similar setting as the first day we brought her home, about two years ago. There is the pumping of the oxygen machine, suction machine and hospital paraphernalia. Things seemed to have changed but not very much!

However, this time there is not an air of hope for future rehabilitation but heavy leaning on the hope of Shelley's future in heaven. It is moments like this that I lean heavily upon my hope and faith that God has prepared a heaven for His children. To think of never again seeing each other after death is the most fatalistic of all views. Thank God for the "blessed hope" we have in Jesus!

Tonight I had the long awaited talk with Shelley. We had alluded to her impending death for some days but I needed to be clear and make sure she was fully aware of her soon home going. I talked and she listened. After each comment I asked her to respond by squeezing my hand. She said she was aware of her serious health condition. She is a fighter so when I asked her if she was at peace with her death she responded, "No". I supposed this is something that God will have to give her. She is worried about the kids after her death and worried about Dan living without his Shelley. So, pray for us and pray for Shelley to receive "dying grace" and inner peace during these closing days.

seemed like a bad dream or a poor joke. They were giving up on Shelley! They were telling me her end is near – she's going to die! I was numb! I was angry at their casual conversation about such a tragic end to a long, hard and tireless battle! They had no clue what price our family had paid over the past two and a half years! And now this doctor was casually giving up on her! And she wanted us to give up fighting as well!

I felt like grabbing Shelley and taking her to another hospital with better doctors and better nurses. I knew about Emory Hospital and its world renowned treatments and cures. Perhaps if I took her there they would have a better diagnosis. They might be able to find us another miracle. But I was tired, weary, weak, numb and beaten. Those many nights of sleeplessness had taken its toll. I was weary from the many battles from arousing her from her coma to battling those nasty infections. I was weary from the aroused hope that things could get better to being devastated when it was another step backward. I was tired to the bone!

Honestly, when you come to the end of such a long journey the caretaker loses strength and yes sometimes even hope to press on. Your body is so weary and your mind is so overwhelmed and clouded from the daily battles that fighting is no longer even an option. But this was not how the story was supposed to end. I had envisioned Shelley coming home and getting better again. I had envisioned Shelley walking again on her own without a walker. I saw the day when Shelley would stand behind a podium and share her story of God's miracle work in her life. That was the story that was supposed to be written. After all, won't this story give God greater glory than an untimely death in hospice?

This time when the ambulance pulled up to the front door of our home there was no hope in the house! Looking back I'm sure that Shelley came back home feeling some sense of relief. I believe hope must have filled her mind. In the past when the ambulance brought her home it was the beginning of one miracle after another. This time it was the end of the story but she did not know.

We decided we would wait until she returned home and all the family was present to sit down with her and relay the painful news. I was still in deep denial that this was the end of the journey.

My son in Dental School in Indianapolis was called home and within a day we were all at home with Shelley under hospice care as a family. She was in a hospital bed and the guest room was once again like a hospital. Hospice delivered the medication to ease her pain and we the family stood by. We were on the last part of the journey and it was the most difficult of all. To watch your wife of thirty years slowly slip away is the worst nightmare one can endure in a lifetime.

This end was far from the way Shelley would have depicted her home going. But being at home with her family was definitely something she would have chosen. Shelley loved her boys so much and her family. I was urged to put her in a hospice care center because it would be so much easier on the family but I would not have it. It was one of my last gifts to my precious wife to have her at home with family when she passed away. So this meant our life would stop and we would await her home going together as a family!

We knew we would see her in heaven again as a family. It was the family giving their final gift to this precious lady. Each day she grew weaker and the nurse told us that usually her patients would die within six to seven days. She visited our home about once every two days to check on her "progress." Medicine was provided to ease Shelley's pain. I confess I had a hard time watching her drift into eternity after the battle we had fought together. It was not a pretty picture watching your wife waste away. While she lay in the hospital bed, I prayed over her for one last miracle of God's grace to release her obstruction but to no avail.

I had learned how to fight over the past two and a half years but now I was being asked to learn how to surrender and do it gracefully. This was the hardest assignment I had been given to date. Every day we would talk, sing, and share as much as possible around the bedside. We finally got the strength to talk to Shelley about going to heaven and that we had fought for her as hard as we could but there was nothing more we could do.

About four days in the hospice journey my son Joshua was caring for his mom when I heard him say, *"Mom wants to say something."* Shelley had lost the ability to talk and communicate over the previous few days. He ran down stairs to get a white dry erase board from the basement so she could communicate something to the family. Shelley did the best she could to scribble something on that dry erase white board that would live etched in my mind for the rest of my life. Joshua said, *"I thought that was what she was trying to tell me!"* On the white board were the words, *"I want one more chance."*

We all wept and cried after seeing her request. She was crying out for life and not for death. She wanted to see her grandchild Luke raised. She wanted to spend time with her kids as she grew old. She wanted another year or two to spend time with her family and her husband. In spite of her handicap and her limitations, she was fighting for her life. She wanted what all of us want when we come down to the end of our life, *"one more chance!"*

But life and the extension of life was not in our hands. We cried, we mourned, we prayed, but we could not provide her request. We felt guilty, we felt broken, we felt desperation, but we could not provide her that, *"one more chance"* that she prayed for. We were helpless to alter the inevitable ending!

And so after seven days at home in hospice our family on March 4th gathered around her bed and we sang hymns and praise songs that Shelley knew. We sang, read scripture, and prayed for her sweet and painless passing into heaven. Our faith had been beaten, bruised, and even tarnished but it still was holding. But our experience had taught us that we have nothing to hold onto without Jesus. In these days we were holding onto Jesus with all our might. In those final hours we were together as a family. I believed it would have been what Shelley wanted. She was in the presence of the ones who loved her so very much!

In the early minutes of March 5th, 2010, at 12:15 AM Shelley breathed her last breath, finished her last lap, and was ushered into the presence of God. She looked at the face of Jesus for the first time, rushed into His arms, and then probably heard her friends and family members calling out her name. People like Elmer Drury, her dad Bob Miller, and her mom Pauline would have been there with open arms. All her friends would have been welcoming her into the greatest party anywhere in the universe. Shelley had finished her fight. And I believe within an instant she was cured of her brain injury. She was once again the Shelley we all knew and loved—smart, articulate, loving, and compassionate. She was healed - eternally healed - and she was walking without a walker.

I can only imagine the conversations they were having at that moment of her home going on the streets of gold. I imagine the joy and celebration of Shelley once again walking, talking, and knowing full health. "What a day that must have been!"

I have full confidence that Shelley is in heaven. Not because she was a good woman, loving wife, and excellent example, but because of her personal faith in the finished work of Jesus for the forgiveness of her sins.

Let me explain how I know where she is. Shelley was raised in an unbelieving household. But a little Wesleyan church and a godly grandmother made a huge grab for her soul. Shelley accepted Jesus as her Savior when she was just a young girl in Sunday school. When her parents wouldn't attend church her saintly grandmother would make sure the three Bob Miller girls were in church. Thank God for people who refuse to let us slide into the abyss. Shelley's grandmother was such a woman. She was feisty, forthright, and unbending in her commitment to make a difference in her son's family.

It paid off! Shelley loved church and soon came to faith in Christ. She grew into one of the leading youth and then went off to Indiana Wesleyan University. She was one of the first in the church to go away to college. She charted new ground that eventually led to other teens leaving for IWU. She's has always had such a powerful positive spiritual impact on people. Many people over the years shared how her leaving the small little Michigan town gave them the courage to leave and go to college.

Before we married, Shelley had set a prayer before God to see her Dad saved. Bob was a good man but not a saved man. She could not think of walking down the aisle without her father knowing Jesus. I remember the day she wrote a heartfelt letter to her dad. When he received the letter it broke his heart. She mentioned in that letter that she wanted to see him in heaven one day and did not have that confidence. Very soon he accepted Christ and became an outstanding believer and church leader. The day she died Shelley's prayer was answered – she is seeing her dad in heaven!

Her suffering and pain over those two and a half years has been beyond comprehension. But I rejoice because as a teenager she trusted Jesus as our savior and forgiver of her sins. There is no more suffering. No more pain! No more hurting hip! And best of all, she has been restored with a clear mind and she's walking on her own.

Every Christian's death should be a road marker pointing toward Jesus. In the final hours, I made a promise to see her on the other side. I know today that Jesus and Shelley must be getting my place prepared. Knowing Shelley, she is no doubt straightening up and organizing something in heaven. Shelley would never be happy just sitting around. Today, she is worshipping around the throne of God and harmonizing with the angels.

In the days that followed we took her body to 12Stone Church in Lawrenceville, Georgia, where hundreds of pastors and laity attended her grand send off. Dr. Earle Wilson, a family friend, preached one of the most powerful funeral messages I have ever heard about heaven. And then we gathered her body and traveled to Delaware as a family. We know this is unusual and many people may not know why we took this step to drive her body ourselves to the burial site. But after I had been so involved in the care of Shelley there was a deep yearning to finish this journey together to the end.

I used my Brother Mark's covered utility trailer and we took her body down to Roxana, Delaware for her final resting spot. It was again a family affair. We laughed and cried thinking about the sight of this family taking this journey. This trip was not financially motivated; it was family motivated. We drove the handicap van and Shelley's body was in the trailer, near her family. We had a short ceremony at Roxana Wesleyan Church on a drizzling overcast cloudy day. My dad, Rev. Atwood Berry, preached a personal heart-felt message that represented the whole family. My mom and dad loved Shelley as much as I did and felt like she was more of a daughter than a daughter-in-law.

Then, Joshua, my son, and I went with the hearse to the graveside at Roxana, Delaware cemetery. We conducted a brief family prayer and Shelley was lowered into the grave. At that moment my spirit was crushed and I clung so hard that heaven was for real. Joshua and I stayed there until the last shovel of dirt covered her plot. We could not give her "one more chance" but we could finish the race and complete the journey. As I stood by that graveside on that afternoon I could hear the words that started this journey a few years ago, *"Dan, don't you go and leave me!"* I was doing everything humanly possible to keep that vow! So I kept my promise until the last shovel full of dirt fell on her grave.

How do you go on living when almost everything you lived for dies and is buried?

CHAPTER FIVE STUDY GUIDE:

1. Discussion: It is amazing how we can adapt to our "new normal" in life. Describe a stage in your life when you had to adapt to a "new normal"?
2. Review the story of the Maryland Blue crab again. Describe a time in your life when you felt like you were stuck in the "basket" and every time you tried to crawl out something pulled you back in.
3. Read the John 6:68-69. Peter asks this question after considering turning away from Jesus, "Lord, to whom shall we go? You have the words of eternal life." Have you ever had a time when you felt like turning your back on your faith? Describe that battle and what got you back on track again.
4. Read 2 Corinthians 12:7, Paul talks about the grace of God that supplies power in the middle of weakness. What does this verse say to you to give you hope?
5. Shelley's favorite quote was, "For every problem there is a promise and for every promise there is a provision." What promises from God's Word sustained you during crisis?
6. Read Revelation 21: 1-5. Describe what heaven is going to be like for the Christian. What hope do we have for our loved ones who die in the Lord?

Prayer:
God I have learned throughout my life that you are enough for everything I face today and tomorrow. There have been times in my life when I felt like giving up but somehow you helped me get through it. I proclaim the belief that you have a promise and a provision for my need today. I stand on your unchanging Word instead of my feelings. Thank you for the hope that I have in heaven; a real place that is prepared for prepared people. I proclaim that that You are greater than anything I am facing today. Thank you Lord for sustaining me today and tomorrow! In Jesus Name Amen!

Chapter 6 Starting on the Path of Healing

"I want God to bless this team so much people will talk about what He did. But it means we gotta give Him our best in every area. And if we win, we praise Him. And if we lose, we praise Him. Either way we honor Him with our actions and our attitudes. So I'm askin' you... What are you living for? I resolve to give God everything I've got, then I'll leave the results up to Him. I want to know if you'll join me?" – Grant Taylor

"No man is wise enough by himself." Plautus

"The remarkable thing is, we have a choice everyday regarding the attitude we will embrace for that day." - Charles R. Swindoll

"If I discover within myself a desire which no experience in this world can satisfy, the most probable explanation is that I was made for another world" – C.S. Lewis

After the funeral we drove home in that same conversion van that we had traveled across Georgia, Alabama, and Mississippi. We now pulled an empty trailer behind that van with an empty and broken hearted driver. Everyone was trying to cheer me and I was trying to dutifully cooperate. Together as a family we did our best to remember all the good and humorous things we could about life with Shelley. Even in our family laughter there was a deep gut level of pain. I knew my life had changed forever and so had the life of my family. How do you heal and move ahead after such a great tragic loss? I did not know and I wasn't sure I wanted to know. But something deep down inside me wanted to stop this painful empty feeling of loss.

Job, the Old Testament patriarch experienced a great loss. Job lost every one of his children in one day. I rejoiced that God gave him back twice what he lost. But now having traveled some of Job's story I ponder these thoughts; did Job ever have a night sitting around the camp fire when the faces of his dead children came flooding back into his imagination? Did Job ever thank God for the now but suffer pain by the memories of what use to be?

My faith says God is in control of everything that happens to us. And I believe that Satan can only do what God allows him to do. And I believe when God allows suffering He makes it work out for my good and His glory in the end (Romans 8:28). But you never forget the face of the loved ones you have lost to death. Maybe Job thanked God for the present but remembered the past with pain. I think that will be one of my first questions for God in heaven!

Just like Job we are not exempt from tornados, turmoil or trials. What happened in Job's life is not the exception to the rule, it is more like the norm of life. Tragedies are the dramas of life that we all live out. It is not a question of if but a question of when. As I drove that van for the last time past the graveside of Shelley at Roxana, Delaware I started an internal dialogue. Maybe it was more of an argument. Do I go on with life or do I just give up? I did not feel I had the energy to carry on. As I steered the van south back to Atlanta I knew which one was winning—the giving up side! It was a debate that would continue to rage for months. I was trying to think of the good that God could make out of this journey but I was hurting too deeply to care. I was tired, weary, worn, beaten, and I felt like just giving up! The caregiver needed a little care! All I could see on that trip south was a husband without a wife, children without their mother, and the world without her witness. I was in a horrible mess!

Men Face Grief Differently Than Women

If you are a man reading this then much of what I am sharing might make sense. Men have a tendency to struggle with grief in a different way than women. Men tend to be problem solvers and fixers. I fought that "fixer" mindset throughout the two and a half year journey of Shelley's recovery. We men want to find solutions to our pain and move ahead where there is instant relief. We have a tendency to try to control our emotions, bury our grief, and rely on our inner masculine strength. During this grief journey I found that many men I talked to about their grief would put a strong steely mask on to hide their struggles. Because they were men, they didn't want to talk about it much and imagined that they were moving ahead when in reality I think they were stuck.

I have found that the men I talked to about their journey shared that they dealt with their grief by getting overly busy at work or doing chores around the house. I know I did this my first year. Some shared that they turned inward and talked to themselves rather than other people about their loss. Some family members mentioned that dad was explosively angry at a moment's notice over the slightest thing. Others have confessed that they poured themselves into excessive use of alcohol and prescription drugs. Men tend to deal more inwardly with their grief and therefore it makes sense that we heal slower.

Take Some Time to Slow Down and Feel Your Grief

I am so thankful for my employer who recognized the severity of my loss and gave me thirty days off to take some personal time for sabbatical and healing. I thought 30 days was too long at first. But I needed the month and more to start healing and establish new habits. It takes time to move beyond the numbness of the loss. And no one can rush grief. And if you have someone trying to rush you into healing and simply getting on with life you have permission to slow down and take it one day at a time. I've been there and I know you just can't rush grief.

I think the depth of our grief is in some way measured by the abundance of our love for that loved one. The greater the love the deeper the hurt! And all of us love differently because we are made uniquely by God. All of us travel a different path because of our own mental and emotional makeup. So slow down! Allow yourself some space and time to think, pray, and catch your breath. Get ready to begin on the journey of healing.

If you are a man you must remember that there are some things that cannot be fixed overnight. It takes time to heal. It takes time to even want to heal. And every man has his own way of slowing down and feeling the grief. As long as there is no harm to yourself or others then start slowly down that path in your own unique way.

Grief Might Be Bigger Than You Imagine

I soon realized this loss of my wife was a bigger giant than I had imagined. Over the past three years I had focused almost all my attention on the healing, rehabilitation, and care of Shelley. I awoke at least three to five times a night so my sleeping patterns were all skewed. I bathed her in the shower every morning of life. I fed her and I took her to the doctors and rehab. My whole life and existence was all about caring for Shelley.

After the funeral I was given permission to sleep all night long undisturbed by anything but my dreams. Even today I find it hard to sleep a full night without awaking. With intentionality I started thinking about myself for the first time in almost three years. At first I felt very guilty. I began to take inventory of my life. I assessed my spiritual, physical, emotional, and relational health. That honest self-assessment was not pleasant nor was the candid evaluation of "failing" in so many categories. Candidly, I was a mess! So, I realized I needed to start on a personal journey of healing.

Those first five or six weeks after her death were horrible times that were filled with sobbing, crying out to God, desires for death, self-pity and anger. There were several nights my weeping was so loud that my Dad would come down and sit across from me in the rocking chair and simply talk me through my pain. He listened and I moaned. I found myself identifying with the Psalmist David when he wrote, "Lord, why are you standing aloof and far away? Why do you hide when I need you the most?" (Psalm 10:1 LB), "Why have you forsaken me? Why do you remain so distant? Why do you ignore my cries for help?" (Psalm 22:1 NLT), "Why have you abandoned me?" (Psalm 43:2 TEV) God seemed so distant many nights. It was hard to believe God had my best in mind when He had stripped me of the love of my life.

With Shelley gone I started to actually move from numbness to feeling again. And what I was feeling was painful and horrible. Not only had Shelley lost her life over the past three years but

I had lost myself over the past three years. I did not know my life without being a caregiver and a helper. I had lived for close to three years with a sense of purpose and was in almost constant crisis. My parents had lived with that same purpose for Shelley and now the object of that purpose for them was gone and it hurt us all. The whole family was trying to figure out how to live life without Shelley!

You Need Someone to Talk Too

One of the major healing times was late night talks. I would not have made it today without those conversations. I believe I know why God spared an 80 year old heart disease and diabetes; it was for those late night soul talks with his son. If anyone knew the pain I had borne for almost three years it was Dad and Mom Berry. I remember one statement dad said over and over again. It was a statement of hope that I did not want to hear at the time. He said, "Dan, you have more life to live, your life is not over, and you will laugh and have joy again."

I remember one night in particular that was systemic in my road to healing. I was setting alone, weeping, looking up at the fireplace and gazing at the family photo on the mantel that depicted

the day of Joshua and Misti's wedding. As I stared into that photo my mind raced back to those happier carefree days. Good days when the family was all together. Grief and pain was nowhere to be seen. A time when our family was fully intact and Shelley stood by my side. What a beautiful family! What a perfect picture! But it had all turned to vapor!

We had so many plans back then. Plans to retire and enjoy our grandkids at our home in Conyers. We had plans to work around the yard together. Plans to sit in that proverbial rocking chair and simply rest together. Then, I broke down in tears. Those dreams were all dashed the day of the accident and they were buried with Shelley the day of her funeral. I remember going through this ritual each night for several weeks and months. I could not help myself from remembering the dashed dreams. I felt imprisoned in my pain!

And with the death of Shelley went all of our shared history. When you have lived together for thirty years you share history and stories. With Shelley, I did not have to go into detail about the stories of Allentown, Western Pennsylvania, Upstate New York, or Georgia. We had lived every minute of life together. My story was her story. Now it was my story alone. There was no one to share those hallowed memories. When Shelley died she took my history with her. Places we had done ministry together! Places we had loved, laughed, and enjoyed living together were forever gone.

Let me describe that decisive turning point in my healing. After many nights, weeks and months of weeping I realized I was facing a serious crossroads in my life. I realized my grief was taking me lower and further away from healing. It was almost as if a voice from heaven spoke to me, "Dan, you have a decision. You are at a crossroads. You can continue to grieve and go downward or you can start digging out for the sake of your kids and grandkids. You know Shelley would want you to carry on!" It was a catalytic moment in my healing. I had a huge internal decision to make.

After what seemed like hours of brokenness, repentance, and surrender, I decided that night to start taking healthy baby steps toward healing. I rejected excuses! I acknowledged to God that this thing called grief was the biggest giant I had ever faced. I realized that unless I sought help I was not going to make it out sane or alive. Grief was dragging me deeper and deeper into self-pity, loneliness, and despair. I truly confessed my inability to handle this thing myself.

I knew God hadn't left me alone. And of course, God hadn't really left the Psalmist David either, and he doesn't leave any of His children alone. He promised repeatedly, "I will never leave you nor forsake you." (Deuteronomy 31:8) But sometimes you feel horribly alone, even in a crowd of friends. You feel very helpless, isolated, and lonely. And those feelings for a man are horrible and not very masculine.

It's Time for Confession

That fateful night I acknowledged before God that I was letting my self-pity keep me stuck in my grief and was keeping me from healing. Grief can take you so low into your pain that you can't dig out. You feel helpless and hopeless. Sometimes you even feel like continuing to stay in the mire of grief to pay penance for merely living. The people that are left behind can feel guilty for life when their loved one is dead. Some people become so full of looking to the past and feeling remorse, pain, and anger they get stuck. Some people even go so low as to pick up a pistol and pull the trigger to end it all.

> **Caring Bridge April 2010:** This past week I met with Pastor Ike Reiggard from the Piedmont Church in Marietta, GA. Ike was a pastor in his 30's when he lost his wife during child birth. It shook him and his faith to the core but it also changed him for the good. We spent about 5 hours together. I found a new friend and loved hearing his stories.
>
> This journey has led me to so many wonderful people I would have never known. Please continue to pray for me as I try to turn my grief into joy. I'm doing everything I can to make sure I am turning outward to help others. I refuse, by the grace of God, to become bitter, sour, or get stuck in grief. I think I owe that to Shelley and Jesus!

I know what the black hole of hopelessness feels like. The day of the funeral, when I stood at the cemetery, I wanted to climb into that hole and be buried with Shelley. My life as I knew it was over! Her death was my death! I can see how some people without hope can actually carry out those plans for self demise. The black cloud of depression is so powerful that it won't turn you loose and it makes you think crazy thoughts. Crazy thoughts that actually sound sane and rational at the time!

During this period of grief a plethora of destructive thoughts flooded my mind daily. I faced the temptation to do selfish acts of condolence. Grief had warped my sensibility. And so I confessed to God all the stuff inside me and asked for help to climb out of the pit.

Dealing with those Destructive Thoughts

In the past, I never understood people who would ponder committing suicide. How could they let pain or grief cloud their sound judgment? In those days after the funeral, I was so far in a black hole that I could rationalize why people who commit suicide made sense. There were long dark nights of despair when suicide really sounded logical. When you are in the depths of despair, crazy and unrealistic thoughts actually make good sense. That is the horrific power of grief and depression. When you get healthier you'll look back and ask yourself "how could I have ever pondered those thoughts?" but it is due to the grip of grief and utter despair. Hopelessness is a horrible thing!

In the grip of grief you don't think about your future, your journey completion, your kids, your grandkids, your witness, your testimony or the fact that God has a story to write with your life. You are utterly and passionately gripped by grief and pain.

Time to Join a Support Group

After battling my demons that catalytic night I looked on the internet and searched all the categories I could find on grief. I saw two options and the first option was a grief support group offered by a hospice at the hospital. I attended two times but soon found that experience less than satisfying. For one they were not permitted to talk about faith or the Bible.

I did not give up because I knew I needed outside help. I found another support group called Grief Share that sounded interesting. I looked for a group near me and found there was one meeting in an evangelical church about 20 miles away. I decided I would try it for one evening. I thought maybe I could find the "secret" to healing from people who had actually traveled the road ahead of me.

About this time I followed up a recommendation by a friend. They told me about Dr. Ike Reiggard and even gave me his book. Ike had lost his young wife and baby during child birth. I read his book first and asked for an hour of his time. Over lunch I tried to find what he did to heal and rise above his grief. Meetings with him were invaluable to the healing process.

So let me recap what happened that pivotal crossroad night. I finally confessed to God that I was stuck in grief. I confessed to God that the journey was too big for me. And, I confessed that Shelley would have wanted me to move forward for me and my son's sake! I still knew that full-time Christian ministry was my calling! I still knew that heaven was real. Jesus said those powerful words, "if it were not so, I would have told you." I believe Jesus tells the truth! I knew deep down that I must make it through this journey and finish my race with integrity!

Count the Blessings of So Many Wonderful People

That night I also reminisced about the journey and the people in the journey of my healing. The song says, "Count your blessings name them one by one. Count your blessings see what God has done." God took me on a mental journey over the last three years of this battle. There is no doubt about it I did not arrive at this place of healing without a team of loving, and compassionate people to pull me through this trial. Without a lot of wonderful people our family would have imploded. The poet John Donne said, "No man is an island." Someone said, "If you see a turtle sitting on the top of a fence post just know that it did not get there by itself." This was true for me as well.

I thought about the support of my loving sons who left their place in dental school and local church ministry to be with us. I thought of my brothers who flew halfway across the country to provide words of comfort and nights of listening. My Mom and Dad decided that their life calling was to be with their oldest son and help him get back on his feet. They took me to the hospital and counseled me through this faith stretching time. They eventually sold their home in Salisbury, Maryland and came to live with me in Georgia. I cannot tell you what family meant to me during this crisis.

I was blessed by friends. A man who heard our story was moved to give financially to help us complete the upstairs apartment. He had never met me nor Shelley and yet God laid this project on his heart. Then the men of a local church who came on many Saturdays and helped renovate the upstairs attic into an apartment for my parents. What would I have done without family and friends.

I am forever indebted to the friendship of a medical doctor that was an answer to prayer one lonely night. He and his wife stepped forward and became our friends and a tool God used over the three years to bless our family medically. And the orthodontist who gave of his services to help straighten Shelley's teeth (braces) after the accident.

And just about the time we were ready to toss in the towel there were notes that came in the mail or email that said, "We are praying for you!" I read each of them over and over and was so comforted by the commitment from others to keep praying. Prayer was uttered all across the country during our crisis.
Several officials from the International Center in Indy came down to replace rotting shutters, vacuum carpets and pray for our healing. They will remember it as a few days helping a friend, and being the hands and heart of Jesus, but we will forever remember it as a salve of healing to our weary bodies fighting a desperate battle.

There was a prayer warrior from 12Stone Church, who saw it as his ministry to stop by and spend hours in prayer and fasting. There was a compassionate ICU nurse who spoke words of faith and comfort. We had a friend who loaned us his car to daily drive to the hospital. Anita, who felt a call to help me in the office and help us organize the many bills. And, for the establishment of a Benevolent Fund that kept us from going under financially. These were acts selfless kindness that people did not have to do but they choose to be an extension of God's grace.

I remember one day when I was fighting feelings of despair. A pastoral friend showed up at the door and brought me the DVDs of "The Real McCoy's". He did not know what he did that day but he kept hope alive in our hearts. And it brought us a few golden laughs in our painful journey.

One day out of the blue a couple called from Oklahoma. They heard about our story and wanted to help. They simply shared that God had told them to come and visit for one week and help us complete the upstairs apartment. They spent over a week; caring for Shelley, renovating the upstairs apartment, and praying for us. They were like angels of mercy and grace that God sent for our time of need. Thank God for these people who responded to the call of God and stepped into our plight to bring grace, healing, and the gift of helps.

I cannot tell you how important it is to have a team helping you through a crisis like we went through. If you are a strong person who prizes their ability to "pull themselves up by their own bootstraps," I promise you, if you live long enough, you will face a crisis big enough, and you will be over your head. You will need a friend, a church and a team.

We really do need each other. When I help you, I don't lose anything. Instead I gain something from the encounter - I gain a friend. When I accomplish a task that blesses someone else, I get a friend who is likely to help in time of need. In addition to that, I have the spiritual satisfaction of knowing I am living out my Christian faith and walking in the footsteps of Jesus.

Galatians 6:2 tells us that "in bearing one another's burdens we fulfill the law of Christ." What this implies is that not only were we not intended to live as lone ranger Christians, but in fact God

> "Life is not neat and tidy. Only in fairy tales does right always triumph. How do we deal with disadvantages, unfair treatment, and injustice? When we can't change our situation, we can change our reactions to it. We cannot change our past, because it stands in concrete. We cannot delete it, but we can learn to see our past from God's perspective. Reject self-pity. Reject revenge. Reject resentment. Reject retaliation. Find ways to discover advantages to your disadvantages."
> - Charles Swindoll

expects us to be there for each other. He expects us to carry each other's load from time to time. His Kingdom demands teamwork. This was demonstrated so vividly during our journey after the accident on September 10th and in the years that followed. In times like these, God uses the Body of Christ to administer grace, hope and faith to those who are hurting. Sometimes these acts and gestures are incredibly timely.

Grief is a Battle for Your Soul and Life

One of my favorite humorous stories is of a preacher in a southern country church. He got up on Sunday morning and preached a scorching sermon about courage, faith, and confidence in God. He told his congregation that they should fear nothing because God is greater than anything they could face. He was greeted with the response of an affirmative congregation.

The next morning the preacher and his deacon went bear hunting. They weren't in the woods long before they found themselves in a precarious situation. It seems a big grizzly bear had been hunting them while they thought they were hunting him. Both men found themselves running for their lives as the big grizzly started running toward them. Both men ran to a nearby tree, climbed the tree, and quickly scurried up out of reach to regain their composure. The deacon said to the preacher, "Pastor, I thought you said on Sunday that we should never be afraid or be full of fear." The preacher responded, "Deacon, I believe that when I'm in a prayer meeting . . . but this is a bear meeting."

Real life is facing those "bear meetings". Our faith is not truly tested until we face the rigors of real life events that stretch us, pull us, and sometimes ripe us apart. What sustains us is when people believe God on our behalf. They breathe hope and faith into during times when we are ready to "toss in the towel." Thank God for those people who kept my faith alive during very difficult days. Like the turtle on the post, I am here today because other's helped me get here!

The Crossroad of Choices

Stephen Covey said, "We are not animals. We are not a product of what has happened to us in our past. We have the power of choice." The choices we make will shape us for the future. We can either remember the hurt and pain or reflect on the blessings. Those choices will either bend us toward good and God or bend us toward pain, selfishness, sorrow, and away from God. That night I sat at that crossroad and I made a decision to move ahead by faith into the unknown of healing. It was my choice!

That was the decision I made that evening. It wasn't easy but I decided to journey down a road of healing. Every one of us comes to a crossroads in life. We can either continue in our mess or chose the road of healing. I tell you it is not an easy choice because the road that leads down the path of least resistance has a strong hold on your life when you are grieving. You must fight and battle for healing every day. But best of all you don't have to travel this journey alone for He has promised, "I will never leave you or forsake you." Maybe God can take this grain of sand called suffering and grief and turn it into a pearl?

CHAPTER SIX STUDY GUIDE:

1. Discussion: Do you think men and women handle grief differently? Why and in what way do you think this is true or untrue? What may be some reasons people try to handle grief/pain by themselves?

2. Read Ephesians 4:16. How is the Body joined together and have a place? How important is being part of a Body versus trying to do life alone?

3. Read John 14:18 and Hebrews 13:5. Describe a time in your life when knowing you were not alone made a difference.

4. Who are the people in your corner when crisis or hard times hit?

5. Have there been occasions when you felt God gave you an encouraging word for someone in trouble? Describe such an occasion.

6. Read Galatians 6:2. How does bearing each other's burdens fulfill the law of Christ?

7. What might be some reasons why people hesitate from starting down the path of healing?

8. What "crossroads" are you facing today or have you faced in the past? What decisions do you need to make to start down the path of healing?

Prayer:
Heavenly Father, thank you for understanding the deepest pains and hurts of our life. We realize our inability to deal with the grief and loss that we face every day. Without you we cannot win the battle! With you we can break out of the cords that hold us in the past. Thank you for friends, family, and others who comfort us. They are an extension of our love to us. We ask you to help us face the "crossroads" of this moment. Help us make some healthy decisions that will lead us forward in the road to healing. In the Name of Jesus Christ we pray! AMEN!

Chapter 7 Two Steps Forward One Step Backward

Proverbs 24:16 – "For a just man falleth seven times, and riseth up again. . ."

"So often in the church today we associate anger, sadness, and grieving with being unspiritual, as if something is wrong with our walk with Christ."
-Pete Scazzero

"God uses broken things. It takes broken soil to produce a crop, broken clouds to give rain, broken grain to give bread, broken bread to give strength. It is the broken alabaster box that gives forth perfume. It is Peter, weeping bitterly, who returns to greater power than ever." – Vance Havner

"You haven't lost anything when you know where it is. Death can hide but not divide." – Vance Havner

"Never give in. Never. Never. Never. Never." - Winston Churchill

"Great works are performed not by strength but by perseverance." - Samuel Johnson

With each passing week, after the death of Shelley, I felt like I was living in a world stained by this human tragedy. On the morning of Friday, March 5th at 12:15 AM, Shelley received her permanent healing from God and left this world to be with the Lord. But what about me? I was left behind to deal with life! I was living a life transfixed on death and dying.

Some days I felt like I was making good progress and then the next day I would be back in the same ditch of grief, depression, and misery. My memory would take me back into the vault of thirty years of marriage, raising the kids together, and so many wonderful occasions when we laughed. Then my mind would race forward to the present and it felt like a hot sizzling iron pierced my chest with pain. This up and down, back and forth feeling was overwhelming some days. So what was the path forward?

Grief Changes Family Dynamics

Dealing with the loss of a loved one is very difficult. Many of you reading this book know what I am talking about. Grief comes in like a rogue ocean wave out of nowhere and more forceful than you can imagine. And when it hits, it can knock you off of your feet. Therese Rando said it well, "Grief is a choppy 'two steps forward, one step backward' experience." This is an excellent description of a rocky experience on the path of healing.

After the death of a loved one the battle is not over. Because Shelley battled for over two years, many thought her passing meant the beginning of my healing. Some people thought that my grieving started on the day of the accident. Looking back I believe I suffered grief in two stages; the day of the accident and the day of her death.

After her death there was a sense of relief and guilt. I felt relief physically that I could once again sleep through the night without getting up to take care of Shelley. And at the same time, I felt guilt that I sensed relief. Strange! What would appear to be relief from this long journey from an outsider's perspective brought greater complexities of emotion. It brought the deeper emotions of despair and guilt. And most of all I was struggling with what I was to become and do with my life now.

Over the past thirty years my whole life was about Shelley and our kids. A few years ago the kids left home, and we enjoyed the privilege of watching them go off to college. Then, it wasn't long before both boys were married to lovely Christian women. There is a deep sense of joy in seeing your kids do what God intended them to do—leave home, find gainful employment, and start raising a family. Those empty nest years allowed us to grow closer together and fall in love all over again.

We did everything together. We worked together, traveled together, and spent an unfathomable amount of time together. Wherever I was – there was Shelley! We were just inseparable and forever more in love and together as we grew older.

With the accident so much of that changed. Our roles changed drastically. Now I was the caregiver and the one provider for every need that Shelley had. I took her to the doctor, prepared her for her shower, fed her, put her to bed, and took care of her like a nurse rather than a husband. But I loved her with a deeper more compassionate love than ever before. Like the past almost thirty years my life was entwined with Shelley.

With her death I was all alone and without a mission. Shelley had become my focus for working and doing life. I had my precious parents upstairs in the apartment that would do anything to comfort my aching heart. Moms and dads are great when you are a kid but I was a full grown adult. As much as they tried to fill that void it just wasn't the same as the marital relationship. Honestly, I had lost who I was and did not know who I was going to be after all these years together. I was a different man than I was when we married in my 20's! If nothing else the last thirty months of caring for Shelley had changed me.

On the death of your spouse you have to acknowledge that you are a different person. The question is, *"Who are you after all these years?"* The person I was when I met Shelley in Allentown, PA was not who I was today. Shelley had changed me forever. Being a father to my boys changed me. My past thirty years of married life had changed the man I was. So, the question for me was *"Who is the Dan who is living in this body today?"* That may sound strange if you have never gone through this experience but honestly, it is that profound.

My answer to that question was, *"I really don't know!"* I was now single and trying to maintain some sense of normality. I was able to keep my job, so there was some sense of financial stability. I was able to keep some of my friends. I found that going from being a couple to being single does not always endear you to your married friends. Things have changed for you but things and dynamics have changed for your friends.

Another thing that changed was the family dynamics. Our accident and Shelley's recovery changed the dynamics of our family. After she returned home to recuperate we soon learned to live a different lifestyle. Everyone knew their role. Mom and Dad Berry covered for me while I did my work. My sons knew they could call and talk to their mom even if she would only speak a few words. Even my sons said on several occasions, *"Dad, even though mom was not the same we became accustom to you and mom being together."* In other words, everyone, including me, had adjusted to our "new reality." It was a horrible reality, but God has a way of helping even horrible to become safe and comfortable. Now, her death meant we were facing another reality; our family had changed yet again.

My boys no longer had a mother to call on the phone, if for only a few minutes. And boys need their mom! My boys did not have a father giving them play-by-play details of another challenging day or encouraging day. They did not have two parents to visit in Conyers but now a single dad left at home. And I think deep down inside they were concerned about who that dad would ultimately become. Things had changed forever!

I remember the first Christmas after her death. We all went to my son Joshua's house in Indianapolis to celebrate the holidays. I don't think the boys could gain the strength necessary to meet back home where mom once lived. The air was thick and laughter came hard as we tried to find a way to now relate without mom present. Life had changed for them as well and it could never again be the same. We did the best we could that Christmas to forge a new family identity.

So let me provide a word of summary. Understand that when you are dealing with grief it is very normal to experience changes in the way you relate to family and friends and in the way they relate to you. Some may distance themselves from you! Others may surprise you with support and a stronger relationship. Because your interests, priorities, or goals may shift you may lose a point of connection in some of your relationships. And surprisingly, you may experience changes in your interests, activities, relationships, and friendships.

Just Get Over It!

One of the things I often hear from those fellow strugglers in Grief Share was the "stupid statements" said by well-meaning friends. Usually the desire of their heart is truly for you to heal, but many times the implication communicated is, *"Just get over it!"* When C.S. Lewis lost his wife he wrote that, *"losing a loved one is like having your leg amputated; the wound may heal, but the leg will never grow back."* You must now learn to live without it. Your life will go on but it will never be the same as it was.

Commenting on his own grief C.S. Lewis wrote, *"part of every misery is, so to speak, the misery's shadow or reflection: the fact that you don't merely suffer but have to keep on thinking about the fact that you suffer. I not only live each endless day in grief, but live each day thinking about living each day in grief."*

A huge part of this process of grief in my life is the daily realization that Shelley will never be coming back to me. The pain subsides to a low burn. Memories bring hopeful encouragement, but at the strangest moments a feeling or a memory can hit hard. It can be a smell, a photo, a place or a voice that triggers it and suddenly I am engulfed in a feeling of overwhelming loss. In a moment the thoughts of just how much I have lost come flooding back! Forever our family has changed. And I ache deep inside!

Habits are hard to break! One morning, I awoke and prepared for the day, like I had done thousands of times. According to my habit, the last thing I did before walking out the door was go to the counter and put on my wedding band. Suddenly, it hit me like a ton of bricks: for close to 30 years that ring has meant that I am Shelley's man and she is my girl. It has meant an eternal commitment. It has meant that we are husband and wife. Suddenly the realization of her death smacked me in the face and I could not help but become emotionally overwhelmed at its impact.

On another day I went to Sam's Club (Shelley's and my place) to pick up a few household items. On the way back to the car, I found myself on the passenger side. I was dumbfounded and disoriented for a moment. Why was I on the passenger side? I realized that for about two years, every time we went to Sam's, I would always take her to the passenger side of the car first, to help her out of the scooter. Now she was not there, nor would she ever be there again. Never again would she occupy that seat. Once more, the grief came flooding back, and the bitter reality of her absence engulfed me.

Throughout the day it was my addiction to call back home and talk on her cell phone. Those few words on that phone would make my day. Now when I called that phone all I got was her answering machine and the clear pre-accident voice from the past. No more phone calls. And eventually I would walk into the Verizon store and do the unthinkable – remove her cell phone from the account. What hurt the most was the loss of her clear strong voice on the other end of that voice mail. When I closed that account I also lost her voice! Little things matter so much!

Some of you who have lost spouses or family members can relate to the impact of these moments. You know about those rouge waves that engulf you at the most inopportune times. In fact, for the first six months I bought sunglasses for my car. Whenever I was out and lost control emotionally I could slip on a pair of sunglasses to disguise my pain and those tears. I just could not endure the possibility of losing it emotionally while out with people. I wanted to be strong!

Regrets or What If's?

After Shelley died, I read as many books on grief as I could get my hands on. I have always been committed to lifelong learning and very quickly realized this journey was way bigger than any "reserves" I had in me. I needed to know more about grief.

One story I came across reminded me about the pain of regret. Thomas Carlyle, was a Scottish essayist and poet who, late in life, married Lady Jane Welch. Not long after they were wed, they found out she had a chronic, terminal illness. He traveled the world presenting his work to adoring crowds. When he was at home, he sometimes focused exclusively on his writing, and he sometimes didn't even see Lady Jane for days on end. The months passed, and eventually, Lady Jane died. She was buried in a country cemetery not far from Carlyle's home.

After the funeral, several friends went with Carlyle back to his house to be with him. He appreciated their friendship, but soon he needed to be alone. He excused himself and walked upstairs to Lady Jane's bedroom. Carlyle sat down in a chair next to her bed. After a few moments, he noticed a book on her night stand. He picked it up. It was her diary. He began to read. Carlyle noticed that on the particular day he came and sat with her, she had placed a star by the date. She noted things like, *"He came by today, and it was like heaven to me! I love him so!"* Carlyle continued reading. On the last day, when she was barely strong enough to write, there was no star in the diary. He read her words for that day. She wrote, *"The day has grown long, and the shadows are up the hall. I've not heard his footsteps, and I know he'll not be coming today. Oh, how I wish I could tell him I love him so!"*

Carlyle immediately got up and with tears running down his cheek, bolted down the stairs and ran to the graveyard where Lady Jane had been buried only hours earlier. A steady rain was falling now. His friends chased behind him! When they arrived at the graveside He was kneeling over the grave, pounding his fist in the earth saying over and over again, *"If I had only known! If I had only known!"*

A painful story? But it tells a story of the horrors of regret after a loved one dies. So many times we have a tendency to beat ourselves up for all that we should have done and did not. I struggled at first but gained some emotional health in knowing I gave it my best to the very end. I realized only months into our journey that Shelley would not be with me for the next decade but maybe just maybe the odds would be in our favor.

I can't say I didn't ask God for one more time to hug her and say 'I love you'. I can't say I haven't thought *"what if I had stayed at the district office on September 10th one more minute."* "What if's" can fill your mind and stunt your emotional health! I realize, however, that I gave Shelley everything I could. Even the day of the accident there was so many times I told her, *"I love you so much."* This knowledge is some sense of relief in my grief. God allowed us time to say what needed to be said. Shelley knew I loved her and I knew she loved me. I have no regrets over words left unspoken, and that is a blessing of unspeakable value. I am so thankful for a God that sustains us even when our life is filled with those emotionally charged "what if's."

I look back often and thank God for allowing me to hear those healing words from our late night talks in bed, *"Dan, stop crying, it was an accident, you couldn't help it."* How I desperately we all need forgiveness, healing, and deliverance from the "what if's" of our pastor.

Sometimes I try desperately to make sense or provide a divine purpose in our journey and her death. When I think about the difficult two and a half years of fighting for her life I ponder, "God, could you have spared Shelley just so I could hear those words of forgiveness?" I don't know the reason but it makes gracious sense to me from a loving God who knows how much I needed to hear those words.

And I suggest to you that if you are dealing with the "what if's" of your loss you'll never find a resolution in your memory. You can play it over and over again in your mind until you go crazy. You can relive those final days and wish you could have been more present, cared more, or said something not said, or have found a different doctor. The bottom line is we all have those "what if's" to deal with. We must give them to God and realize we did the best we could with where we were and what we had. Forgive yourself! Forgive others! Turn it loose and let God start healing you!

Joy in the Mourning

Part of the healing process of grief is learning to smile and laugh again. It is part of "two steps forward!" God wants to turn our "mourning into joy." On one particular day God gave me a healing lift that would continue to provide a salve for months. It may even put a smile on your face.

I had been working way too hard, and failing, to take my day off. Remember, I said I used work to keep from feeling. One morning I decided to relax a little and do some target shooting. I drove to a nearby church that is in a rural area of Conyers, GA. The church has about 50 acres and I had been given permission to shoot my rife and pistols and do target practice, so I took along my 38 special and a 22 rifle with scope. I simply wanted to relax and shoot a few rounds with my rifle. Dad Berry went along with me and took his old 32 pistol to shoot a few rounds as well. His pistol was one that hardly worked and he was hoping that cleaning and oiling this antique would ease his mind about firing a few rounds.

My dad took out his pistol and started to show how well his special care had worked. After only two pulls of the trigger it was jammed again. Imagine an 80 year old man struggling with this pistol to get it unjammed. It was an accident waiting to happen! What we didn't know at that time was the ammunition was a "hotter" round than was recommended for that old relic. It was a wonder it did not explode in his hands.

I was having a ball. I had shot about 50 rounds when I heard a yell coming from behind me. To my surprise I saw a Rockdale County uniform officer with a Glock pistol pulled pointing at us. He was serious! The officer had his pistol drawn and he meant business. I had watched enough TV crime stories to realize I needed to throw down my pistol and raise my hands high above my head. Surely this was a misunderstanding!

But Dad was oblivious to the officer's command. He was standing there waving his pistol around trying to clear the weapon.

I yelled at dad to drop the weapon and point the pistol down at the ground. He was hard of hearing and he continued to wave the pistol around with his back turned to the officer. He was fully unaware of the danger of the moment. It was a bizarre site but a serious encounter. Like the criminals in "America's Most Wanted" I threw my hands in the air. I yelled out, "Whoa! Whoa! We're just target practicing, I have permission to be here, and I have a weapons permit to carry." I wrestled the pistol out of Dad's hand and threw it on the ground as well. Then, to his surprise he looked up and saw the officer for the first time.

If only there was a video camera to record this scene! Two preachers with their hands raised high in the air. Weapons on the ground! Fear in their eyes!

The officer wanted to know who we were and what permission we had for shooting. It took about 30 minutes and I had to call the local church pastor to verify who I was and that I had permission to be on the property. I honestly thought we were going to be arrested.

I later found out that one of the church members called the police when he heard the sound of gun fire on the property. It was a running joke for months.

If this story doesn't put a smile on your face, well you just might lack a sense of humor! It was a day of laughter but also a reminder that God spared us from greater danger.

What I've found in this journey is that even in the most heavy and difficult times of crisis, God has a way of lightening the load. Many times He does it through unexpected moments of laughter. These moments have a way of ministering to us in times of grief like nothing else can. Sometimes they become the very things that help us keep our sanity. God is a gracious and wise God who knows exactly when a good laugh is just what the doctor ordered.

So as I close out this chapter let a fellow struggler suggest a few suggestions you might practically apply for moving ahead in your healing.

1. **Take each day and each obstacle one at a time.** Rushing your grief is like trying to climb a flight of steps three steps at a time. You are bound to stumble and fall head long. Give yourself a break and take this grieving part of the journey one step at a time. You will overcome and save yourself much hardship by simply focusing on the one step in front of you today!

2. **If you fall don't feel you have to start all over again.** For every leap forward, there's been a stumble backward—sometimes just an inch, and other times, what seemed like miles. Grief has its good days and bad! Keep pressing forward! Don't give up! Don't focus on the flops but the inches forward! Even the smallest healing step needs to be celebrated. If you fall, get back up and start right where you are!

3. **Don't let guilt debilitate you.** When you have a bad day it is natural to feel debilitated and disappointed. You have a choice; to let the frustration throw you into the cycle downward or resolve to move forward. That step backward can cause you to feel like giving up or you can simply accept the step back and say, "I'll get up and move ahead!"

4. **Give yourself a break.** Sometimes our worst enemy is ourselves. We make life a matter of black and white; winning or losing. Much of life and grief is lived in those grey or neutral areas; it is no one's fault. It is what it is! So stop blaming yourself and give yourself a break. For every peak, there is a valley. We grow when we do our best to learn from and move beyond our challenges instead of obsessing over them and making ourselves feel stuck.

5. **Moving forward is painful, expect it to hurt!** Just like a muscle needs to tear to grow stronger, sometimes we need to wade into our own darkness to find a brighter light. We don't need to worry that every setback indicates something's wrong with our healing. So long as we're making progress on the whole, we can trust we're doing just fine. It won't be pain free but we will be making progress. Anticipate the pain of a grief group, getting outside of your comfort zone, meeting new friends, going to counseling, and a

thousand other "painful" steps forward.

6. Let yourself laugh again! Relax along the journey and learn to laugh again! Give yourself permission to smile and look at life again through fresh eyes. Stop beating yourself down and know deep down inside you can make it!

CHAPTER SEVEN STUDY GUIDE:

1. Discussion: Have you experienced the "two steps forward one step backward" that is described in this chapter? How did you respond? How has your relationships changed since you have suffered your loss or grief? How have you changed since the loss? How are you different today than what you were before suffering?

2. Proverbs 24:16 says, "For a just man falleth seven times, and riseth up again." How hard is it to keep on moving forward when you fall? What has helped you the most to get back up and start forward again?

3. The chapter describes not having regret about spending time together. Which of these have you struggled; "regrets" or "what if's?" How are you moving beyond these feelings?

4. God has a way of providing those moments of cheer and humor in our journey of grief. Share a time when humor helped you through a difficult or painful circumstance.

5. The chapter provides six helps for dealing with the "two steps forward and one step backward" days. Go back and review those six helps and respond as to which one is the most helpful to you personally today?

Prayer

"Lord, there are times when I feel like I am climbing out of the pit of suffering and pain and then only to fall backward again! Lord, I need your help today to keep on believing and keep on trusting when the journey seems uphill and impossible. I want to heal! I want to see the good around me! I want to look for the signs that you are sustaining me daily. I want to see the good in my journey instead of the dark clouds. Help me to start looking upward to what you want to do in me and through me in this journey of grief. In Jesus Name, Amen!"

"No one knows the tears still inside me. People think it's all past. They think I'm all better.
Every once in a while I think, I hope, I pray that things will be better too. But then I remember.
And the pain floods back, and the bottom falls out, and I fall and I fall. And I know once again that things aren't all better. My loved one is gone, and I cry alone. How much longer, God? How long does this last?"
-Kenneth C. Haugk

Chapter 8 Looking For A Higher Purpose

"Wide awake to the presence of God, I realized I had been so focused on asking why a good God allowed bad things to happen that I was missing out on the nearness of God all along. In becoming preoccupied with the why, I was missing the Holy Who of God's presence." –Margaret Feinberg, Wonderstruck

"Worry is putting a question mark where God has put periods." – John R. Rice

"Precious in the sight of the Lord is the death of His saints." – Psalms 116:15

"God is His own interpreter, and He will make it plain." – William Cowper

"To the child of God, there is no such thing as an accident. He travels an appointed way. Accidents may indeed appear to befall him and misfortune stalk his way; but these evils will be so in appearance only and will seem evils only because we cannot read the secret script of God's hidden providence." – A.W. Tozer

"God marks across some of our days, "Will explain later." – Vance Havner

I sat across the Subway restaurant table from a seasoned pastor. The first words out of his mouth, while wiping tears from his tired eyes were, "Dan, why did it happen to her and why now?" He had every reason to cry out in brokenness with the age old question, "why?" Only a few hours earlier his wife, daughter, and her boyfriend were involved in a serious car accident. It came in a macabre and strange sort of way.

The group was on a selfless trek to purchase school supplies for her sister's kids. As their family car drove down a two lane country road, a pine tree fell on the car. There was no storm, no driver error, no strong winds, nor a cloudy sky. This huge pine tree fell out of the blue on this lone car. Bizarre! It didn't make sense then and it still doesn't make sense today. There was no rhyme or reason to this horrible accident. The only member hurt in the car was the driver; their daughter. She was struggling for her life in intensive care with an injury that could leave her at best paralyzed for life. The doctors informed the family that her injury was the same injury Christopher Reeves endured. But this is not the full story! About four years earlier I was called to visit the hospital after this same daughter had been involved in another accident. This accident was beyond critical. Her brain was protruding on the outside of her broken skull. She hung onto life by a thread. They called me to pray for wisdom and God's miracle. The doctors had presented the organ donor papers for them to sign at her impending death. When I arrived at the hospital there were two other pastors there and we joined together to pray over this comatose body. We prayed, trusted God, and God miraculously and sovereignly answered prayer. She awoke within an hour of that prayer and started moving her hand and communicating. Within a few days she was taken to The Shepherd Center to continue her fight for recovery. Her rehab would take years battling injuries and handicaps.

The first accident didn't make sense but this second accident was credulously unexplainable. How does a loving God allow a rotting tree in an isolated woods to fall upon a single car and hit an already injured and handicap girl? Her mother did not understand and told me and God, *"Why wasn't it me?"* Her brother and sisters did not understand and offered themselves to God as a worthy substitute. I had no plausible explanation then and I don't have answers today.

In the days ahead his daughter would undergo surgery to repair her C1 through C3 vertebrae in her spine with a long metal rod. She would again face weeks and months of rehabilitation. She would return to the same rehab center as she had four years earlier to fight the battle. Why her? I don't know why her! And why now, after all she had gone through? I don't know! And no matter how smart, wise, or biblically literate you are – you don't know either. Some things in life are unexplainable!

This is the type of story that causes the atheist to smile with glee and say, *"I told you there is no God and life doesn't make sense. We are spinning on this planet called earth and it is out of control. Life is chaos!"* In moments like this, sitting across from a broken hearted friend in Subway restaurant, we may be tempted to believe that maybe God doesn't know, care, or is powerful enough to act before we experience such horrible pain.

Is it wrong to ask why?

I asked those same questions through my journey with Shelley many times. *"Why would God permit this to happen to Shelley?"* and *"Why now God?"* God did not answer those why questions for me and He may not give you a full insider's view of His rationale for your "whys." I would not expect an answer. And if God were to give you one, it may still not make sense. There are some things in life that have no clear answers on this side of eternity. Some things are best left explained in heaven and until then we either trust Him or reject Him.

The gospel song writer Charles Albert Tindley says it well, *"Trials dark on every hand, and we cannot understand all the ways of God would lead us to that blessed promised land; but he guides us with his eye, and we'll follow till we die, for we'll understand it better by and by."* The song writer was so accurate in describing our trials and challenges down here as beyond our ability to understand. So we look to eternity and wait until the unknown becomes known, the questions fade into answers, and until the tangled threads are seen through the perspective of God. So we will understand it better "by and by." But what about the "here and now?"

Sometimes we feel like God is pulling against us.

I heard of the story of a guy who was driving up to a mountain lake, and on the way up, it starts snowing. He gets out and installs the chains on his tires. While he's doing this, another car comes along and slams into his car. And he watches in horror and disbelief as his car bounces over a rocky cliff and burst into flames.

He continues trudging up the mountain on foot, in the snow and sleet, and he's getting sick from the cold. Then, as he rounds a corner, he sees in disbelief that his cabin has burned to the ground. He starts hitting his head against the wall, and asks, *"Why me, God?"* The heavens parted and a booming voice speaks, *"Because some people just tick me off."*

117

That story sounds more like the Greek legends of Thor and Zeus than the God of the Bible. But, I think most of us have questioned one time or another, *"Maybe what is happening to me is due to God punishing me."* Maybe my grief is due to something I did in my life or some action I have taken. Why would a God who is all-good, all-knowing, and all-powerful allow these bad things to happen to me?

These feelings must be basic to the human condition because the Psalmist in 22:1 felt those same exact feelings and wrote, *"Why have you forsaken me? Why do you remain so distant? Why do you ignore my cries for help?"* In Psalms 43:2 it says, *"Why have you abandoned me?"*

The good news is God loves us and is on our side.

God does not hold a grudge against us. He loves us in our pain, confusion, and questions. The Bible says there is no condemnation for those who are in Christ. He is pulling for you and not against you! He loves us with an unlimited love. His compassion is new every morning and His forgiveness is without fail. Take courage God is on your side! Apostle Paul said in Romans 8:31; *"If God is for us, who can be against us?"* (NIV) Be assured of His love for you today! Where is God when you hit bottom? He's right there underneath you. In Deut. 33:27 it says, He is *"your refuge, and his everlasting arms are under you."*

One day the disciples were out doing ministry with Jesus. One of the disciples saw a man who was blind and asked the age old "why" question. In John 9:2-4 it says,
"Master," his disciples asked him, *"why was this man born blind? Was it a result of his own sins or those of his parents?"* *"Neither,"* Jesus answered. *"But to demonstrate the power of God."* (TLB) There is something within us that wants to understand the complexities of life and the rationale of purpose. Jesus gave them an answer and allows us to listen into his explanation, *"to demonstrate the power of God."*

A few minutes later Jesus takes some mud and places it over the blind man's eyes and instructs him to wash in the Pool of Siloam and the scriptures tell us, *"So the man went where he was sent and washed and came back seeing!"* (Jn9:7 TLB). In this story Jesus healed the blind man and he left rejoicing. But even after meeting Jesus and experiencing his healing power; one day the blind man died. And one day even the best cure will give way to mortality. That is just the way life and death is for us humans. The statistics are overwhelming; 100 out of 100 people die!

During the thousands of years since Jesus walked on planet earth Christians have died rather routinely at the mercy of dictators and despots. In Hebrews 11, the mood changes from an essay on deliverance to an essay on martyrdom. It provides a list of those who died without being delivered from the executioner. *"Others were tortured and refused to be released, so that they might gain a better resurrection. Some faced jeers and flogging, while still others were chained and put in prison. They were stoned; they were sawed in two; they were put to death by the sword. They went about in sheepskins and goatskins, destitute, persecuted and mistreated— the world was not worthy of them. They wandered in deserts and mountains, and in caves and holes in the ground. These were all commended for their faith, yet none of them received what had been promised. God had planned something better for us so that only together with us would they be made perfect."* (Hebrews 11:35-40-NIV) So, take hope that God is for you even when you hurt and are feeling broken and estranged!

We pray for God's deliverance and receive God's providence. Vance Havner described a time after he lost his wife of thirty-three years where he went through a deep valley of depression and grief. In his journey out of grief he wrote these words, *"When before the throne we stand in Him complete, all the riddles that puzzle us here will fall into place and we shall know in fulfillment what we now believe in faith - that all things work together for good in His eternal purpose. No longer will we cry, 'My God, why?' Instead, 'alas' will become 'Alleluia,' all question marks will be straightened into exclamation points, sorrow will change to singing, and pain will be lost in praise."*

119

It all boils down to faith and trust in God. Do you believe in your heart that in spite of your pain and grief - God is a good God? Do you believe that in light of heaven this life on earth is but a dot in comparison? Do you trust God that "all things are working for our good and God's glory?" Can you allow time for those questions marks to be straightened?

The prophet Isaiah had an interesting perspective on the knowledge and wisdom of God. He said about God, *"For my thoughts are not your thoughts, neither are your ways my ways, saith the LORD. For as the heavens are higher than the earth, so are my ways higher than your ways, and my thoughts than your thoughts."* (Is 55:8-9 KJV) There are so many things in life we fail to fully comprehend. I do not understand how the internet works but I depend on it every day. I do not comprehend satellites and space technology and yet I receive its benefits every day of my life.

But not every person maneuvers the path of adversary, pain, and death the same way. Some people sincerely want to know what God is up to in their life. And when answers do not come promptly they run from God. Some people become bitter, hardened and callous because they see God as the author of their pain and grief. In the end once we leave God and the safety of faith we have nowhere to turn.

Let me give you a few statements about the, "why God?" that may be helpful for you honest seekers of truth. These are statements that represent the last few years of sorting out my personal walk with God in this area.

1. God never promised that He would answer all our questions.

We beg for the reason why because we want to make sense out of something that is complex and unexplainable from our perspective. From our perspective, God taking our loved one seems so arbitrary and nonsensical. If God would just show us His higher and nobler purpose then we could more easily release our loved one to God. We would be relieved knowing how the puzzle pieces fit together. But that is not God's way! We ask for "why" and God seems silent. We cry out for purpose and God gives us solitude in response. It is our humanness and our selfishness speaking when we ask "why!"

I remember hearing years ago of a mother who was doing a needle point of a picture. Her little six year old daughter was sitting on the floor watching. All the daughter could see was the tangled pieces of fabric from the underside. Her mom promised that when she finished knitting she would bring her up on her lap and show her what she was doing. So after an hour her mom lifted her up on her lap and she saw from her mom's vantage point. It was the colorful picture of a beautiful landscape. All its details were in perfect color and symmetry. This little six year olds mouth dropped open with amazement of its supreme beauty. In many ways that will be our expression in heaven – a jaw dropping awesome experience at how all the pieces fit into place.

2. **Pain can blind us to the answers to our prayers and the omnipresence of God.**

Some of those long difficult days and nights when I was at my wits end, I did not see or feel God. But because I could not see or feel God did not mean that God was not with me. The mere fact that I am here today is a living testimony of the grace of God upon my life. In essence he was, "carrying me" during those days. Feelings can change, but faith sustains! In Matthew 27:46, even Jesus felt the absence of His Father when he was on the cross. He cried out, *"My God, my God, why have you forsaken me?"* (NIV) If Jesus felt that absence from his heavenly Father, then grief will inevitably make us feel a distance from God. But be assured He is there "carrying" you.

Corrie ten Boom and Betsy ten Boom were Christians who lived in the Netherlands during World War II. They hid Jews in their home to protect them from the Nazis. When they were discovered, not only were the Jews taken to the concentration camp but Corrie and Betsy were taken as well, and they spent the rest of the war there. After watching one atrocity after another, Corrie told Betsy, *"This place is the pit of hell!"* Betsy replied, *"There is no pit so deep that God's love is not deeper."*

3. God is at work in ways we cannot comprehend.

During this grief journey God was developing my inner man and my faith life. As I look back, I can see how I was fully dependent upon God in so many ways. Doctors, hospitals, treatment, and people failed me often. I was learning to depend upon God in ways I had never depended before. C. S. Lewis, who watched his beloved wife die of cancer, put it this way: *"But pain insists upon being attended to. God whispers to us in our pleasures, speaks in our conscience, but shouts in our pains: it is his megaphone to rouse a deaf world."* It is only in hind sight that I can see His amazing fingerprints of love and compassion in this journey.

4. We live in a fallen and corrupt world.

Our ancestors came from the Garden of Eden where life was perfect—no sickness, pain, and suffering. There was no cancer, heart disease or sin. When sin came into the world it corrupted this world and mankind has been looking for a return to Paradise ever since. Oh, for that perfect world where there is no more tears, pain, and suffering. A place where there is no more frailness of the body and mind. C.S. Lewis described this world we are living in today as *"always winter, but never Christmas."* I must accept the fact that this world is not perfect until God redeems this fallen state in the climax of history.

5. Knowing the reasons why will not take away pain from grief.

Let's be candid, if God were to show us all the reasons why He allowed something to happen in our life, would it heal our pain? No, it would probably mean more questions for most of us. If we got our questions answered we would immediately have six more questions needing answers. Deuteronomy 29:29 says, *"The secret things belong to the LORD our God."*

6. We were made for heaven.

If all we have is life down here on planet earth then we are most helpless. The materialist believes that life here is the primary focus. The atheist believes when you die we return to dust and are mere food for worms. But to the people who believe and have trusted God through Christ for their sins forgiveness, we believe there is more to this world than just what we see. I believe that we are body, soul, and spirit. I believe that my soul will live on in eternity and one-hundred years from today I will be alive in the presence of Jesus. *"My end,"* said, Mary Queen of Scots, *"is my beginning."* Queen Mary was certain that there was an existence beyond planet earth, and I do as well.

7. Faith builds as we learn to trust our past, present, and future with God.

At Shelley's funeral, Dr. Earle Wilson preached a powerful message from John chapter 14. In that message he mentioned these poignant statements from Jesus, *"If it were not so I would have told you."* Jesus was asking His disciples to trust His word and His promise to them. Do you believe that Jesus is a liar? Do you believe that there is anyone who has walked on earth that knew more about death than Jesus? C.S. Lewis said it well, *"You must make your choice. Either this man was, and is, the Son of God: or else a madman or something worse. You can shut Him up for a fool, you can spit at Him and kill Him as a demon; or you can fall at His feet and call Him Lord and God."* I had to come to the conclusion that Jesus is who He said He was – the Son of the eternal God.

There is a song sung by Babbie Mason called Trust His Heart. In the song it says,
"All things work for our good; though sometimes we can't see how they could.
Struggles that break our hearts in two; sometimes blinds us to the truth.
Our Father knows what's best for us; His ways are not our own.
And the chorus says,
So when your pathway grows dim; and you just can't see Him.

Remember you're never alone; God is too wise to be mistaken.
God is too good to be unkind; so when you don't understand.
When you don't see His plan.
When you can't trace His hand.
Trust His heart!

8. We are all living between Good Friday and Resurrection Easter Sunday.

Today as I type these words it is Saturday. It is the Saturday between Good Friday and Easter. We call it Good Friday because we know what is coming in two days—Resurrection Sunday. Saturday is the day that is between promise and fulfillment. It is the day when it seems we are all in a holding pattern awaiting Sunday and resurrection.

In the Bible, Saturday was the day the high priests and Pharisees gathered together before Pilate and asked him to have Jesus' tomb sealed. Saturday was the day that Jesus made His descent, whereby He destroyed the gates and bars of Hades. According to Ephesians 4:8, death was put to death. Hades was stripped of all its captives. The forefathers and all the righteous who died from the beginning of time were set free. All of this was happening on Saturday – the in between day.

If you were to ask the disciples on Saturday what the future of that feeble band of believers was, you would have gotten a frail response. You see, it was Saturday, the "in between" day. Everything was looking bleaker than Good Friday, when they crucified Him on the cross between two thieves.

What gives me hope in my grief is that you and I are living on the edge of Saturday awaiting Sunday. Our loved one has gone on before us. Our hopes and faith has been tested to the breaking point. This is the "in between" day or phase of life. But we are assured that it will end with the celebration of a glorious Easter Resurrection. And, this resurrection is the great cornerstone creed of the Church in the Apostles Creed, "I believe in the resurrection of the body." And it is more than a spiritual resurrection but a physical one. R.A. Torrey writes, "We will not be disembodied spirits in the world to come, but redeemed spirits, in redeemed bodies, in a redeemed universe."

So, until I see God face to face and get my questions answered, I trust Him for a noble and high purpose. I have learned that pain can blind me to His presence. I have learned that He is working in ways I cannot comprehend. I have learned I am living in a fallen and corrupt world. I was made for heaven. I have learned that I need to trust Him with my future, and best of all, I am living "in between," awaiting Easter resurrection.

CHAPTER EIGHT STUDY GUIDE:

1. Discussion: As you look back over your life, describe some events or crisis that has caused you to ask God "why?" Have you ever felt like God was against you or punishing you for past sins?

2. Read Romans 8:1 and Romans 8:31; what does it say about God being on your side?

3. What difference does it make in your life when someone believes in you?

4. Read John 9:2-4; why do you think the disciples desired to know "why?" What does it mean when Jesus said, "to demonstrate the power of God?"

5. Read Hebrews 11:35-40; what one word comes to mind when you think about the full list of Hebrews 11 and then read the list of those who died for their faith?

6. What does the author mean by the statement, "We pray for God's deliverance and receive God's providence?"

7. Go back and review the list of insights the author learned in his journey dealing with the "why's" of his wife's death? Which one speaks the strongest to you and why?

Prayer:

"Heavenly Father, I confess today that I don't understand why things have worked out in my life the way they have. I confess that I have felt lonely and by myself in my journey. But I also confess that I know that you have not left me alone. My feelings may change but your promises remain. I ask you to help me grow in my trust for you each day. Help me to surrender myself into the will of my Heavenly Father. God, I take confidence in the truth that heaven is real and my future awaits in eternity with my friends, family, and Jesus forever. Amen!

Chapter 9 Understanding the Journey of Grief

"When you're grieving. That's not the time to be brave or strong. You need to let it show. If there were no love there would be no grief." – Zig Ziglar

"I don't want to be here 17 years from now. I want to heal." – Roger Spradlin

"God never wastes our sorrows. Self-sufficiency is a terrible place to be. We need God." – Joseph Stowell

"I think God is far too faithful to let anyone make it through life without confronting seasons of utter helplessness." -Beth Moore

Hang on tight because grief is a powerful and complex force to battle. Grief is defined as, "a deep mental anguish, as that arising from bereavement." At the core of grief is this thing called "loss". Anytime we lose something of deep value we deal with some facet of the grief process. The loss of a job, divorce, retirement, declining 401, or health issues can trigger some phase of grief.

But the death of a loved one is the most difficult grief journey you will ever face. It is more than the loss of that person, but loss of your identity and your own sense of value and worth. It will take you years to sort out just all you have lost when a spouse dies. When Shelley died I lost more than my wife. I lost an accountant, a manager, a bookkeeper, a salary, a referee for our family disagreements, a counselor, a ministry partner, and a precious friend. The losses continue to add up every day of life!

No two people handle grief the same way. Sometimes the death has been expected for months or even years, so there has been time to deal with the eventuality of that person dying and leaving you behind. You may have planned the day in your mind, what you would do, and how you would handle it. But I assure you that the actual moment of finality still brings shock waves. It may send you into another grief cycle. It may not be as severe as the loss of a loved one from suicide, accident, or illness that lasted a second, minute or week but it is still tremendous pain and loss. Never put a pain value on someone's loss. How we process grief is individual to us alone!

As we mentioned in the last chapter, it is natural when suffering grief to want to protect one's self from the agony of dealing with the loss. You feel cheated and want answers to why this has happened. Sometimes you struggle with those "what if's" and "if only's". What if I could have done something more? Of feeling there was something you could have done to have prevented the death. Sometimes there is anger at God or family members who did not respond as graciously as you would have hoped.

For me I struggled for at least one year with asking myself, "what if I had broken the rules and physically taken Shelley to Emory Hospital?" I wondered if they would not have been able to operate on her bowel obstruction or done something to prolong her life. These thoughts can haunt you and even drive you to feelings of insanity.

Naturally if you have some concerns about the spiritual life of your loved one you will deal with the question, "I wonder where they are in eternity?" We cannot know what went on in the silence of the heart of a loved one before they died so we best leave that question with God. All I know is that God's character is eternally loving, just, and fair. God does all things well.

We may struggle with anger. Sometimes the thought of them getting to go to heaven and leaving us behind brings the pain of separation. We cry out to God, *"Why didn't you take me instead of them?"* I remember vividly standing at the graveside in Roxana, Delaware. Beside me that day stood my youngest son who needed his dad. But I was selfishly wishing I could jump into the six foot hole with Shelley and end life all together. There was nothing more to live for after her death. I didn't even know how to do life without here. Thirty years is a long time to live, serve, and love each other. There was deep anger that I had to go on with life. The thought of going on without her was beyond comprehension that day.

128

Let me assure you that feelings of grief are normal and very natural after the death of a loved one. It is not a sign of weakness or sickness. When you feel the tears coming and your mind tells you to be strong, just relax and let the tears flow. Don't hold them back. They are healing tears. Tears are God's way of letting you continue the healing process and empty your soul of pain.

I have talked to people who fought the tears and the grief process. Then one day something small is the catalyst that opens the flood gate of pent up grief. Grief will either mend you or you will break under its force. Don't pretend you are fine when you know you are not. Share it with a friend who will listen. There are no feelings that are out of boundaries to share. I remember that Jesus cried when his good friend Lazarus died so it is alright to cry.

Understanding what is Happening In You

The foremost authority on the study of grief is Dr. Elizabeth Kubler-Ross. Her landmark book titled, On Death and Dying (1969), provides the core of most literature on the complexities of the grief process. She categorizes the grief process into five simple stages but I want to add one more for those who are people of faith.

1. Denial: Kubler-Ross says this is a natural reaction to the shock of the news. The feeling that "this can't be happening to me." I remember hearing the news from the doctor that Shelley would not be getting better. The doctor spoke about hospice and I simply refused to hear the word. The thought that Shelley was being admitted into hospice and she was going to die did not sink in for hours. I was thinking to myself, *"Maybe the doctor went to the wrong room and got Shelley mixed up with another patient."* I thought to myself, *"Maybe this doctor doesn't know what she's doing. I think I'll get a second opinion."* We all go through denial, trying to come to terms with the horrible news. Usually at this stage we tend to shut down and not want to talk about it. We find it difficult to audibly speak the words. What we all need during this time is a friend to listen quietly and assure us of their concern and compassion.

2. Anger: In this stage we start to think about taking action. Part of that action is to become angry at other's around us. It can be directed at our family, doctors, and even God. There is a feeling of such utter desperation. We are trying to deal with the unfairness of it all. Truly if God is all-powerful, why has He allowed this to happen to me? This is especially true if the person has been a faithful Christian and served God well. Such anger is unpredictable but not necessarily sinful. Job expressed his anger this way, *"Therefore I will not keep silent; I will speak out in the anguish of my spirit, I will complain in the bitterness of my soul"* (Job 7:11). I remember feeling that God had let me, the prayer partners, and our family down. After the long hard battle with Shelley's illness how could God let the story end this way? I vacillated between denial and anger for several days and weeks. Each of these stages are not a neat progressive stage upward but more cyclical and repeated over time.

3. Bargaining: This is where we start trying to make a deal with people around us, doctors, the hospital, and God. This is where most people are willing to do anything or make any pledge to see life extended or the end to change. I remember promising God that if he would raise Shelley out of her hospice bed that I would take her around to churches and share God's story of healing. I have heard of people who have promised to live better, give generous gifts, or see projects through to completion before death. This is all an attempt to delay the inevitable acceptance of the reality of a loved one's death or dying. What I needed more at this stage of grief was simply a friend who would listen to my rants, feel my pain, and understand the pain behind my harsh words. I didn't need simplistic and pity answers to the unexplainable mystery.

4. Depression: Eventually the stage called depression hits us. Someone said, "depression is anger turned inward." When we can't succeed in denial, anger, or bargaining we have to face our loss. Or, it could come as we face the reality of mounting hospital bills and funeral expenses. Depression can grip us as we face the future being alone. We might think about the future affairs, paperwork, children, and a litany of worries. When depression comes sweeping into your life it can have physical and emotional impact. I have seen people so affected by depression that they experience physical changes, suffer hair loss, and gain or lose weight. When the reality of death hits us, eventually we must all deal with some facet and degree of depression. During this stage it is helpful to have a friend to listen, provide comfort, but also gently help you get unstuck. Depressed people want to run from company, friends, or activity. I remember some friends inviting me out to dinner, a movie, and activity just to get my mind off of myself and my pain.

5. Acceptance: This is not necessarily a happy time but it is a healthier stage of the grief process. Emotions may flow and anger may be present but the conversation is now changing. There is a coming to terms with the idea of life after the death of your loved one.

All through the funeral experience I was dealing with all five stages of Grief. But standing around the rim of that grave and seeing that casket for the last time was a final acceptance for me. There was nothing more I could do!

We had chosen to rent a trailer and take Shelley's body back to Delaware as our final act of togetherness as a family. Together in life and together at the time of her death! Although we had ridden together as a family to her burial site we would be going back to Georgia alone. A painful acceptance of our new reality!

For those of you who have a faith that your loved one is in heaven with Jesus. There is a sixth stage that Dr. Elizabeth Kubler-Ross did not include. But this last stage is the greatest constant comfort for me.

6. Christian: Hope. At the heart of the Christian faith is the hope of resurrection. The Apostle Paul told the Christians in Corinth that had Jesus not been raised from the grave, our faith would be totally futile (1 Cor 15:12-19). But on Easter, God did indeed raise Jesus from the grave (15:20). All Christian hope resides in the One who was once dead, but who now lives forevermore. The hope Christians have is that death, though a real enemy, will not have the last word. The resurrected Christ has the final word, and it is the word of eternal life. The Christian hope and promise is that this frail, failing, mortal life will, in the resurrection, take on immortality through Jesus Christ our Lord (15:35-49).

For Christians, the hope of the resurrection is a word of comfort. To those who are not Christians, the hope of the resur-rection is a word of invitation to repent of their sins and receive the Redeemer as their own. For believers, we have the confidence in a future hope. Jesus promised, *"I am going there to prepare a place for you. And if I go and pre-pare a place for you I will come back and take you to be with me that you also may be where I am."* (John 14: 2-3) This is hope for

the person ready to die and for those who are left behind.

So, how do all these six stages play out in the healing process of grief? Over the years I have found that everyone goes through these stages differently. Not everyone goes through every stage of grief the same. The stages are not always in the same order. You may notice that you may regress from time to time to an earlier stage. I have provided this visual depiction of the way I experienced grief. To me it was like an upside down tornado funnel. At first the phases were slow and painful (large end of funnel). Then over time they became more muted and easier to deal with and less severe and long. Everyone progresses through the stages at their own pace. You can't force people to move on.

Give yourself permission to grieve the loss of your loved one. It is alright to cry, moan, question, get angry, not get angry, turn inward, retreat, or explode if it is all done within healthy boundaries. God already knows what is going through your mind and your emotions and still loves you. God knows the questions you are asking in your mind so verbalize them to Him in prayers of brokenness.

I find that many men have a difficult time with grief because they don't want to be seen as losing their masculinity. But if Jesus, the man of all men, could cry at the loss of his good friend Lazarus, then we should not be concerned about tears and expressions. Tears heal the heart and empty out our feelings of brokenness.

Men want to fix it and make it better by nature. Men are by nature doers. We want to find a quick solution to the ache in our heart and move ahead. By design God has made us providers and protectors. This natural tendency does not work well when dealing with grief. There is nothing we can fix to make it better. We can't bring our loved one back. We can't fix our heart from hurting. We can ignore the grief but it keeps coming back stronger until we acknowledge our brokenness and allow God to start healing our broken heart.

I heard the story of Will Randolph Hearst's castle that has stuck with me for years. He was a very rich and powerful man that that always had a strange and unusual demand for his house guests. Whenever he entertained guests he had one banned subject for all patrons. They were forbidden to discuss or talk about death! His parties were restricted to conversations about Hollywood, politics, and entertainment. He was a man living in denial of the realities of life. The statistics are fairly overwhelming; 100% of the people living will die.

Real life is not about burying our fears, concerns, or life's realities. Part of living in the real world is dealing with a world that is filled with death and brokenness. I think most men dealing with grief can relate to Randolph. We want to fix our grief and stop our pain because God made us that way. We want to live in a world where we could do something to make it stop hurting and to bring back life as we knew it before.

Many grievers try to avoid the realities of the loss. Don't run! Stand firm and hold on tight. Grief is like riding a wild bucking bronco. It may take weeks, months, or years but you can work through this. I cannot tell you the scars of the loss will ever disappear, but God's grace is sufficient to get you through this journey and back into life and health perspective.

Know when to get professional help! I know after the death of Shelley that my mind would drift on occasions to death and suicide. Being tempted is normal. Thinking about the "easy way out" – suicide – is part of the battle. In fact, every 41 seconds someone commits suicide to attempt to ease the pain of their depression. And every 42 seconds a family is left behind to deal with the aftermath of this "solution." Think about your family, your friends, your testimony, and your God. Suicide is not a solution, it just creates a larger problem and horrible pain for everyone you leave behind.

I have talked to people who were so close to committing suicide. They told me when they were at their wits end they actually had talked themselves into believing that suicide made the best sense. Suicide added up as a wise decision. If that describes you then you need to get help today. By all means, if suicide has become the focus in your mind, talk to someone about your feelings. Tell someone you need help and get help!

You Will Smile Again! I can distinctly remember a particular evening. It was one of those evenings when my attention had turned to the family photo of Shelley and our boys. The photo was taken when Jason, our oldest son, was getting married to Amber. It was a photo of happier days when life felt so easy and fun by comparison.

As I gazed at that family photo my mind began to race back to what a wonderful life I had before the loss of Shelley. We had an awesome marriage and a great family over these past 30 years. I thought back to how when the kids had left the house that our marriage had gotten better. It was all about us focusing on our marriage. We now had more time for building, growing, and maturing our relationship. Everything by comparison was "perfect" back then.

Then, I felt the stab of pain in my heart for the great loss. I can remember breaking down in loud wails of agony. I thought I was going to die under the pressure of grief. My heart was going to be crushed under the pain. My wails were so loud that Dad Berry came downstairs to try to help ease my brokenness and pain.

Setting before me was a 79 year old senior trying to comfort his first born. He had deeply loved Shelley as well and so there were tears in his eyes. He listened to me with compassion. He let me pour out my pain, grief, anger, injustice, and brokenness without a word. He just sat and listened. He would wipe a tear from his eyes every once in a while as I ranted on in pain and my grief diatribe. The conversation must have lasted several hours.

Then the conversation grew quiet as I sit and wiped my eyes with half a box of Kleenexes. I had talked myself out. I had cried until there were no more tears. Then he looked long and deep into my face with the love of a father. From the other side of the room he spoke words of faith. *"Dan, I know it does not seem possible tonight. But one day you will smile again. This too shall pass. God is not finished with you yet. You have many more good years of usefulness for Him. You will have joy again. I know you don't feel it tonight, or maybe tomorrow, but believe me, you will smile again."*

I wish I could tell you my response was admirable, but it was far from that. In my heart I rejected his words in anger. But I sure needed those words. Here he had given me his best words of comfort, and inside my heart his words fell on a hard heart. I felt pangs of hurt, rejection, and anger. I silently said to myself, "He doesn't know what pain I am enduring." All I could see that evening was a very heavy dark curtain of grief that separated me from that faith statement. Surely he did not know what he was talking about. There is no way that I could ever again smile, feel joy, or return to any former happiness.

Believe me life can get better. Trust me, grief will not always have a hold on you like it does today. You feel you will never rise out of this pit but you can, and you will. You feel you have nothing to live for, but you will feel differently in the days ahead. Hold on to that bucking bronco! Refrain from turning inward and retreating in depression. Keep pressing forward and don't give up.

Over my years of ministry I have known many people who have shared their story of the "former life." I love to hear testimonies from people who lived hard and callous existences until they came to know the forgiving and healing power of Jesus Christ. I can remember more than one who told me their story of God's grace, but also showed me their scars from the journey. They have a face that is darkened, broken, and cracked by a hard life of suffering and sin. Their tattoos label them as part of a gang they had once served. Knife scars dot their body from bar room fights they had survived. In other words, they had come out from the past by the grace of God but the scars of the past still were visible on their body.

I believe that may be the story of my life and perhaps yours. My scars are not visible to most eyes but they emotionally grip me from time to time. The scars allow me to point people to where the grace of God has brought me. The scars are proof that I have been where you are or maybe going. The brokenness may subside and the grief may gradually ease up. One day you will smile again but you will probably point, from time to time, to a scar or two of the journey.

So for those of you looking for help in your grief let me offer you a few simple suggestions from someone who has been in the fight of his life.

Believe, "You can survive grief." I wish you had a compassionate dad like I did in my grief but if you don't, let me speak hope into your life. You can face this huge battle and survive it and even thrive afterward. I know you don't believe me right now but it is true. You must believe today that God loves you and has a plan for your life. You must believe that your final identity will not be defined by your loss but something far more. Until HE is finished with you, keep living, keep pressing forward toward that purpose.

Don't run from your grief, lean into your grief. The temptation to run and cover it up is great, but don't. Lean into the grief like a swimmer facing a huge wave. Brace yourself and lean into the loss. Don't cover it up, don't become callous to the pain but embrace your grief and lean into it. Keep talking to your friends and keep active. Refuse to retreat and hide from humanity.

Believe that you will eventually get better and start to heal. I know you may not feel that way today but you will in time. Don't rush it but allow God's Word to once again give you assurance on the joys of heaven and the blessed hope we have in Christ. You will get better, just give it time. Time will start to heal the brokenness, pain, and deep hurts.

Remember that people will say the stupidest things - forgive. During my journey I have met the most loving people with the ability to say the most outlandish statements. They actually thought they were helping me. I have had people suggest I should search for another spouse at the funeral of my wife. I have heard people say, "It was for Shelley's best." These words hurt painfully! You want to respond to their insensitivity but please refrain. They simply don't know what they are saying. Give them grace because most of them actually leave the visit with a smile on their face thinking how helpful they have been.

Communicate to people what you really need. If you don't tell them they won't know, so share what would be the best way to be a blessing. If you need space then - tell them. If you need food or friendship - tell them. If you don't want more meals brought into the home - then tell them. Unless you communicate your needs adequately then people won't know how they can help. People really do care and want to help they just feel at a loss for what to do – so tell them.

137

Postpone all the big decisions until you are healthier. Dr. Earle Wilson said to me privately at the funeral, *"Dan, promise me that you will wait a year before you make any big decisions."* I made that promise and I'm glad I did. People will suggest you need to downsize the house – wait at least a year. People will want to help you with your finances or invest your life insurance policy – wait a year. People will ask you to sell or give them something you think you may no longer need – wait a year. Someone will come along offering you the possibility of a new marriage relationship – wait a year. Don't be rushed, pushed, or pressured. Because of the tenderness of your heart you need time to heal and to also get back some sense of clarity of thought and wisdom again.

Seek wise counsel if you need affirmation to your progress. Within a month of Shelley's passing I felt from time to time like my grief was not healing as quickly as I supposed it should. I was still dealing with some thoughts that bothered me. I questioned my own healing progress. So, I sought out a professional counselor. It cost a few dollars but it was worth the investment. Over the years I have been fairly active in counseling so I realized how the sessions worked from behind the curtain. I walked into the first session and shared with him everything I felt and every emotion that crossed my mind. I was as open and venerable as I could be to the counselor. I held nothing back. I might have confessed something I wasn't even feeling to help the counselor get to the heart of the session. I guess you could say; I wanted my 50 minute hour and my investment to count!

He asked for another session and I was more than willing. After the second session he set back in his chair and spoke these words, "Dan, you want to heal faster than grief will allow you. You are making progress but it is not as quickly as you desire. Keep going to your small group sessions on grief and don't come back unless you need to talk."

This may not mean anything to you but that night I left having been affirmed. I was not going crazy and what I was feeling was natural. He affirmed that my path to healing was on track and I was doing everything humanly possible I could do – except patience.

Keep putting one foot in front of the other. Keep stepping forward toward healing and health. Grief can immobilize you and leave you like a deer starring into the headlights of an oncoming freight train. So, take the car out of neutral or park and put it in drive. Even first gear is alright. Realize that there is no better time than today to move forward. Reconnect with some old friends. Accept God's comfort, love, and healing.

It is so easy to allow grief to become your identity. You become so trapped in your grief that you think of yourself only through the prism of loss. When people see you they have a tendency to run away. Your whole life and conversation is one about your pain. Getting stuck in your grief is not a compliment to your loved one it is an illness you must identify and start on the path of wholeness. Loss will become your identity if you don't move ahead by putting one foot in front of the other.

So, let me give you permission today to start healing. God loves you! God knows the depth of your pain! Your loved one would want you to move ahead. God has a plan for the future of your life. There are people who you can help! Start putting one foot in front of the other by doing something even today that will move your identity from grief to joy.

Just recently I let my father, who is now 83 year old read this chapter. He smiled about the part of that conversation that fateful evening. But he willingly asked me if I would insert this message to YOU. So, if you don't have a father or friend to speak them to you take it from my dad and I believe your heavenly Father.

"_____, I know it does not seem possible tonight. But one day you will smile again. This too shall pass. God is not finished with you yet. You have many more good years of usefulness for Him. You will have joy again. I know you don't feel it tonight or maybe tomorrow but believe me, you will smile again. I believe in you!"

CHAPTER NINE STUDY GUIDE:

1. DISCUSSION: Where are you or your friends on the chart of the Six Stages of Grief today? Have you ever experienced a loss that related to the stages? Share your story!

2. What is the greatest personal temptation that has come out of your grief?

3. Review the list, which grief life lesson has been the best help to you?

4. Why do you think people have a tendency to get stuck in grief and can't find their way out?

5. The best way to deal with grief is moving away from self-pity. Read I Thessalonians 5:18 and reflect on what it means to thank God in all circumstances.

6. Christian hope is one of the greatest means of gaining comfort in your loss. Read I Corinthians 15: 12-20; 35-49; John 14: 2-3. What comfort do you find from these verses about heaven and eternity?

7. How are you doing with your journey of Grief?
   a. Do you have someone to talk to?
   b. Do you have a friend who will listen to you?
   c. Are you moving healthily through the stages of grief?
   d. Are you seeking to find a fresh sense of meaning and purpose?
   e. Are you releasing the past and finding new interests?
   f. Are you waiting on those big decisions until at least a year?
   g. Are you spiritually healthy and growing in your faith?
   h. Are you starting to remember the past and celebrate the good?

PRAYER:

"Lord, you are a good God and a gracious God. I ask you to help
me to heal on this path of grief. I don't want to get stuck in my
grief by self-pity. I don't want my identity to be wrapped around
grief. I want to heal and I want to smile again. Help me God to
believe that I can get through this darkness called grief. My grief
blinds me to the things around me that are good. Open my eyes to
see things that are good, hopeful, and encouraging. In Jesus Name,
Amen"

Chapter 10 Permission to Get Unstuck

"There is a compassionate adaptability about God's will for us. Because we have not been in God's special will for us from the beginning, there is no reason why we should not get into it now. He can take up from where we get right."
"The sorest afflictions never appear intolerable, except when we see them in the wrong light." – Brother Lawrence
"I have found that if we go as far as we can, God often opens up the rest of the way." – Isobel Kuhn
"Whenever I haven't known what to do, I've just tried to do what comes next, to take the next logical step by faith." – Robert J. Morgan

Queen Victoria was the ruler of England but life came crashing down when her husband, Prince Albert died. He lay sick in bed for several weeks and then succumbed to typhoid fever. He was only forty-two years old. His death on December 1861 left Queen Victoria in deep depression and mourning. From that moment on her life was changed forever. Her deep love for her husband seemed to grip her beyond the normal pattern of grief. She stayed in seclusion for many years, rarely appearing in public. She mourned him by wearing black for the remaining forty years of her life.

Albert's death came suddenly and unexpected. She wrote to her daughter Victoria shortly afterwards: *"How I, who leant on him for all and everything—without whom I did nothing, moved not a finger, arranged not a print or photograph, didn't put on a gown or bonnet if he didn't approve it shall go on, to live, to move, to help myself in difficult moments?"*

From the time of her husband's death, the Queen's mourning became her major focus in life. Her very existence was wrapped around mourning. The Prince's rooms in their residences were maintained exactly as he had them when he was alive. Her servants were instructed to bring hot water into his dressing room every day as they had formerly done for his morning shave. She had statues made of him, displayed his mementos around the royal palaces, and she spent most of her time secluded in Windsor Castle or in Balmoral up in Scotland, where she had formerly spent so many happy times with her husband.

After the first year of mourning the people in Britain saw the Queen's mourning as an obsession. There was some gossip about her even seeking a spiritual medium to make contact with her beloved Prince. Her state of mind was questioned and her absence of attendance in public events began to wear thin on the people.

We read of this painful obsession and we sympathize with her tragic loss. If you have lost a loved one you can relate to at least some of those deep feelings of loss. We all know someone like Queen Victoria who has become obsessed with grief. She will not be the last one that has become stuck in their grief.

I remember a few years ago when my mother-in-law lost her husband Bob Miller. He was outside mowing grass when he was stricken with a heart attack. The ambulance was called and he clung to life for only a few minutes. When the family arrived at the hospital they informed them that Bob was dead upon arrival. For months Pauline was in a deep state of depression; she would not venture outside the home and had to be motivated by her friends to go out to dinner. Over the years it became her obsession. Every conversation included the name of her beloved husband and my father-in-law. We all loved Bob but Pauline could not move forward. She was stuck in her grief. It was only a few years afterward that she contracted cancer and joined Bob in heaven. I wonder sometimes if her death was not due to her focus on her beloved Bob.

Getting stuck happens all the time to people who have lost a loved one. They become so focused, broken, and myopic about their lose that they are frozen in time and pain. The death of their loved one actually defines who they are for a long period of time or in some more acute cases, for the rest of their lives. They seldom heal and mature beyond the time of the death of their spouse. Their remaining life is defined by mourning and death. This black hole, called grief, has pulled them down into the abyss and they have lost the power to go forward. This is what I define as, "being stuck" in grief.

Death is as normal to life as birth.

We are all going to face a time when our existence on planet earth will be over. Steve Jobs, founder of Apple, in a 2005 commencement address at Stanford University shocked many secularists. He had been diagnosed with cancer and although he had fought it bravely, the end was in sight. So he spoke with some sense of foreboding when he said, "No one wants to die. Even people who want to go to heaven don't want to die to get there. And yet death is the destination we all share. No one has ever escaped it. And that is as it should be, because death is very likely the single best invention of life. It is life's change agent. It clears out the old to make way for the new. Right now the new is you, but someday not too long from now, you will gradually become the old and be cleared away. Sorry to be so dramatic, but it is quite true."

"Most people journeying through grief have a sense that although the terrain is difficult and frightening, at least they are moving through it, however slowly and erratically. What they're experiencing is painful, but the nature and intensity of the pain changes from day to day. For people who get stuck, nothing seems to change. It's as though the death happened yesterday." - Phyllis Kosminsky

I appreciate Steve's reality but I disagree with Steve's philosophy about death being a great invention. Death is the mortal enemy of mankind and in I Corinthians 15:26 it describes death as, *the last enemy to be destroyed.* Until our parents, Adam and Eve, sinned in the Garden of Eden we would have lived forever, but sin changed all of that. One day on Calvary Christ took care of our mortal enemy death forever. Christ's death, burial, and resurrection is our ultimate proof that there is hope beyond the grave. Without Christ we truly are hopeless and eternity will be more than a "clearing out." The songwriter said it well, "Because He lives I can face the tomorrow, because He lives all fear is gone." So, while death and life are normal it is not God's perfect plan for our life.

Mourning is a normal part of dealing with death.

When we lose a beloved spouse or family member it is normal to grieve the loss. The length of time of grieving is rightly different for every one of us. There is no exact amount that is considered ideal for everyone. Everyone grieves at their same pace but the intensity of grief should be decreasing over time. Sometimes people will tell you to, "get on with life" as if you could put aside the years of relationship and love. You can't move on at will, but you can move on over time if you desire to get healthy.

Every culture has its own way of dealing with grief. Today people still dress in black and pull their cars to the side of the road when a hearse drives by. In some cultures they start with black at the funeral and then over a period of time the attire of the grieving moves through the various stages of grief by color. Mourning moves from full black to half mourning grey, and then the color lavender before coming out of mourning. The way people pay their respect and honor the dead differs from the north to the south and east to the west.

Mourning has a place in our life. It allows the family to respect the memory of their loved one that passed. It also gradually gives permission for those that are mourning to adjust to life and the, "new normal". To mourn is natural and healthy. Our customs allow us the time we need to begin to deal with a new start for the grieving family.

Sometimes mourning feels like you have fallen and you can't get up.

We have all seen the TV commercial of the elderly lady who has fallen. In desperation she cries out, "I've fallen and I can't get up." Mourning can feel like that "fallen" feeling. We cling to the memory of the past and can't move beyond it. We feel as helpless as Queen Victoria to get back upright and move back into the land of the living.

146

I have heard stories from missionaries of how they catch monkeys in some parts of the world. They employ an ingenious method to catch them. They use a large heavy jar, with an opening just big enough for the monkey to squeeze a hand through. In the bottom of the jar, they place a banana as bait. The monkey slips its hand into the bottle and grabs the banana. Then, holding tightly to the banana, it is unable to remove its hand from the jar. It never occurs to the monkey to let go of the banana, so it remains in the trap by the jar.

Memories can be healthy but when those memories grip us so tight that we can't move ahead then it is not healthy. Like the monkey, we cling desperately to the memories, smells, photos, and images of our past life. We feel a distinct sense of honor and duty to preserve our memories. So we cling ever so tightly, only to find that we are captured by the very thing that we love. The greater we loved, the deeper the pain of the loss. If only the past could be reclaimed! So, we cling tightly to the memory of a lost love, a lost spouse, and a lost dream. We feel helpless to turn it loose and move toward healing. In holding it too tight we are trapped by our love and memory and we can find ourselves stuck in our grief.

> "These past few days I have experienced the deepest grief and sense of loss I have ever known. Yes, I believe strongly in God, His Word, the promise of our resurrection in Christ and heaven. I affirm those truths. And they do comfort. But I was not prepared for the depth of pain I am experiencing. I thought I was somewhat prepared as Carol had fought cancer for the past five years and 10 months. But I underestimated how severe this grief would be." – Dr. Jim Garlow on the death of his wife Carol

Mourning can be very painful and debilitating

Grief has a greater impact on us than just the emotions. Grief is manifested emotional, physically, spiritually, socially, and intellectually. There are no parts of our life not affected by grief's grip. Because it is all encompassing, it sometimes overwhelms the grieving.

Physically: Grief can make you feel exhausted and anemic. It can change your eating patterns; eating too much or too little. It can cause digestive problems, diarrhea, and weight loss or gain. Headaches, chest pressure, and heaviness can persist for days. Your muscles can tighten, body pains increase, or feelings of weakness. It can change your sleeping patterns where you sleep too much or have disturbing dreams. Your doctor may prescribe a mild sleeping aid to allow you to restore healthy sleeping patterns without addictive problems. You should refrain from using medication as a long-term solution unless recommended by your doctor. Grief can have a radical physical impact on your life. Don't hesitate to see your doctor for a full physical and allow your physician to assist you in your healing.

Emotionally: There are emotional stresses that can make you feel like you are going crazy. These feelings are unpredictable and different with people. You may feel up, down, dizzy, overwhelmed, calm, or all over the place with your emotions. It may feel like you are going crazy with the roller coaster ride of emotions. As long as your emotions are progressing you are on the right track. Most people talk about feeling numb and in disbelief. This is a normal defense mechanism of your loss. When the numbness wears off you will feel the full weight of grief. Everyone must eventually deal with the full shock wave of reality. People describe feeling sad, crying, and then not able to cry. There may be feelings of relief and guilt. If your loved one has been sick for a long time then there may be a sense of relief followed by feelings of guilt for feeling relief. If you were involved in an accident you may feel, "survivors guilt". You may have regrets that you are alive and your loved one is dead. You may feel regret over the feeling that you could have done more to help your loved one. These are all normal feelings for those who are dealing with grief. The spectrum of emotional feelings run the gamut; fear, anxiety, anger, relief, guilt, and worry.

Relationally - Suddenly your relationships have changed. Especially if you have lost a mate and you are now single. You may not be comfortable being a single around your other married friends. Then you begin to look around and say, "Where have all my friends gone?" Socially your life has changed. Then, there are bizarre feelings that cross your mind or fill your dreams. Feelings that sometimes scare you and make you think seriously about your health. If you feel like you need help then by all means don't hesitate to talk to someone. Talk it out with a friend, your pastor, or a counseling professional. I believe it is best to talk to a professional counselor because they can see you without bias or filters. Sometimes just knowing that you are doing well under the circumstances can be reassuring. If you need help don't hesitate to seek out someone and talk it out.

Spiritually – There are spiritual challenges! During grief most people report that they feel lonely and disconnected spiritually. God can feel like He is a million miles away from you at times of grieving. It is not abnormal to cry out in desperation, "Where have you gone God?" Many deeply committed Christians have shared the difficulty of hearing Bible verses quoted to them during this time. What has been a solace in pre-grief days has now become a bitter pill to swallow. What a grieving person most needs from their spiritual family is the ministry of presence and prayer. Sometimes just listening and sitting quietly can be the best source of help.

Why Do People Get Stuck in Grief?
While all of these emotions are normal after the loss of a loved one, over time these feeling should become less intense. For some people this happens in a few months and for others a few years. It is normal after you lose someone you love to continue to feel sad. However, in normal grieving it doesn't stay in the dominate focus of your mental life. One of the indicators that you are stuck in your grief is when grief has become the dominate focus of your life and shapes your existence. You are stuck in grief if grief has stepped onto the center stage of your life and will not take a bow to exit. When grief is the dominating factor in your thoughts, conversations, and dreams, then you are stuck. When your conversations always seem to revolve around your story of grief, then you just might be stuck.

There are several reasons why grief can hold you in its grip and not want to release you. Read over the list of the twelve symptoms below and see if there are any that has become dominate in your life. Circle the ones give you the most problems.

1. Focusing on the lost alone
2. Not changing your former patterns and create new patterns
3. Living in the myopic past
4. Locking yourself away
5. Letting depression breed
6. A sense of disbelief or denial regarding the death long after it has occurred
7. Recurrent pangs of emotions with intense yearning for the dead loved one
8. Avoidance of situations and activities that are reminders of the loved one
9. A preoccupation with distressing thoughts about the death
10. An intellectual understanding of grief but helplessness to feel better.
11. Increasing irritability and anger.
12. Self-destructive behavior; drinking, substance abuse, or promiscuity

How Can I Get Unstuck from my Grief?

1. Take a personal inventory of your grief. Do you really want to get out of the pit of grief? Do you want to be emotionally healthy again? I know the question sounds insulting but healing begins with a deep sense of honesty and confession. In John 5: 1-7 there was a man who was an invalid and was lying next to the pool in Bethesda. He said he wanted to be healed. He had been "stuck" in his condition for thirty-eight years. Jesus asked him a powerful question, *"Do you want to get well?"* The man's reply was descriptive of his emotional condition. He said, *"I have no one to help me into the pool."* In other words, this man was waiting for something

outside of himself to lift him in the pool for his healing. He basi-
cally blamed his circumstances and the people around him for not
helping him get healed. This man was stuck in his condition!

**2. Allow the memory to be healing and not debilitat-
ing.** There is something within all of us that wants to keep the
memory of our loved one from fading. But if that fear of forget-
ting is too strong, our compassion becomes our captivity. Are you
fearful that the memories of your loved one will fade away if you
give yourself permission to heal? Because Shelley's death came
two and a half years after our accident there were times when I was
unable to remember the good times and instead was constantly
tormented by the bad ones. All I could think of was the suffering,
the hospital stays, the last days in hospice, her gasping for breath,
and her desire to live and be with her family up until her death. My
thoughts frequently turned to self blame and questions. Why hadn't
I done more for her? Why hadn't I gotten better treatment that
last month? Many questions have no answers, and they just made
my pain worse. There came a time when I had to put aside the bad
memories and focus on the good memories. The days before the
accident. The times when our family was whole and healthy. I
had to trust that those good memories would outweigh the painful
ones.

It will be very important for you to take personal responsi-
bility for your path to healing. You can't blame being stuck in grief
on your friends, family, or colleagues. You have to desire deeply to
start moving forward or you will stay stuck in your grief. I personally went to see a private counselor to confirm that I was making
progress. I also stayed with a support group my first year of grief.
If six months or more has passed and you feel you are stuck, then
don't hesitate to join a grief support group or see a professionally
trained counselor or psychologist. Remember that grief will take
you deeper than you imagine and last longer than you anticipate.
Give yourself adequate time to heal.

3. Realize you have to do your part in the healing process.
Someone said it this way, "God doesn't move parked cars." It is normal for everyone to face the initial shock of grief. It is normal to go through a mourning process of weeks and months. But it is also healthy that you begin to lose the initial intensity of grief. For that to happen you have to be personally engaged in the healing process. You have to make a decision to move forward in your healing. At some stage you begin to realize it is not healthy to live in the past and that God has a hopeful future for you.

For me my moment of decision was one evening simply looking up at the family photo with Shelley and the boys. I realized deep down inside that it was up to me to start the healing process. No one could make the decision to get serious about my healing but me. I realized that for the sake of my family, friends, and my devotion to God that it was time to start putting the pieces of my broken life together. It was not a lightning bolt experience but a decisive moment for me and it can be for you. Everyone needs a moment where you simply confess, "I am sick and tired of being stuck! God help me move forward!"

4. Get out of the spotlight of grief. Grief can become addictive without even knowing it. Grief can bring about the emotion of self-pity! If you stay in grief without growing then grief will define your relationship with people and friends. Grief and self-pity begins to feed a new identity. I have seen people so stuck in their grief that they unknowingly were feeding on the sympathy, attention, and self-pity of their condition. You start enjoying the benefits of being supported by others. I know it sounds difficult to believe, but some people can become addicted to the attention of grief. It was about six months in the healing process that I made a conscious decision that I did not want grief to become my identity. I hope you will make that same decision when it is time!

5. Start reconnecting with others. There is something about grief that pulls you into depression, isolation, and loneliness. Grief feeds upon itself in that dark atmosphere! Pause and think of all the people around you that need you to heal. There are family members, friends, and relatives that are waiting for you to discover your new destiny. Get up today and seek out someone with whom to go to lunch or supper. Walk around the mall or Wal-Mart and make it a point to talk to people (and don't mention your loss). Call someone who lost a loved one and comfort them! Find someone who is hurting in your neighborhood and go do something nice for them (like others may have done for you). There is no better time than now and no better day than today to kick start you path out of "stuck."

6. Deal with those destructive thoughts and attitudes that are keeping you down. Feelings of anger, bitterness, and resentment will keep you face down on the mat of grief. No one grieves perfectly and without some need for an attitude adjustment. Because you may be wrestling with your relationship with God, you will need to meditate upon the basics of faith. Maybe you feel that God let you down because your prayers for healing or protection were not answered. Remember afresh that God loves you! In spite of what you feel embrace His forgiveness and love. Learn to trust God and His providence and give your loss to Him. Give your, "whys" to God and rest in the knowledge that God is good and knows what He is doing. Give your anger and bitterness to God! Anger is not neutral and can affect every area of our life. Give your anger to God!

Start daily to repeat faith thoughts that will help lift you up. Thoughts like, "I may feel like I can't go on but I know I can by the grace of God!" or "I believe that God is giving me daily the strength to go on!" Monitor your thinking and your emotions. You cannot alter your circumstances but you can alter the focus of your emotions and your conversations.

7. Decide you will reinvent yourself into a new you!
Before the death of your loved one you lived, worked, played, and experienced life in a certain way. Now you are different and life has changed forever. You can't go backward but you can move forward.

For that to happen you have to discover the new you. Who are you now? What new interest do you need to pursue? You will probably find that you have different friends and maybe even different interests. Your loss does not have to define who you will be in the future. Decide you don't want to be known for grief but for joy! Give yourself permission to heal and move beyond your old identity of grief to a new identity of hope and joy. There is a new you that God wants to birth inside of you that will be filled with joy once again.

> "I thought I could make a map of sorrow. Sorrow, however, turns out to be not a state but a process. It needs not a map but a history. Grief is like a long valley, a winding valley where any bend may reveal a totally new landscape." – C.S. Lewis

The author of Hebrews gives an example of what I am talking about. It says, *"If they had been thinking of that land from which they had gone out, they would have had opportunity to return. But as it is, they desired a better country"* (Heb. 11:15-16). Instead of bemoaning the loss of comforts in the previous land (as the Moses-led Israelites did many years later), Abraham's people trusted that God was leading and blessing them. For Abraham, the "promised land" was more than a new place in which to dwell, it was also a reality of mind and heart, reframing life in the belief that God had called him to a significant new life.

As sure as God called Abraham to a new land and a new life, God is calling you to discover a life outside of the downward spiral of grief. If God did it for Abraham he can do it for you. If God did it for me He can do it for you.

The rest of the story in John 5 tells us what Jesus did for this invalid man who was stuck in his condition. It says, John 5:8-9 *"Then Jesus said to him, "Get up! Pick up your mat and walk." At once the man was cured; he picked up his mat and walked."* I believe that God may be speaking your name and calling you to pick up your mat and begin to walk. Trust me, it may not be easy but if you will simply take the first step toward healing God will help you take the next step.

CHAPTER TEN STUDY GUIDE:

1. Discussion: Do you identify with Queen Victoria on the first page of this chapter? In what ways have you felt her story was like yours or perhaps different from yours?

2. Review the list of eleven "stuck" identifiers. Which of the eleven is your greatest battle today? Which ones have you moved through over the past weeks and months of dealing with grief?

3. Have you ever been angry at God for something you feel He did that hurt you or someone else close to you? How did you deal with those feelings of anger?

4. How did anger at God affect your desire to attend church? Read your Bible? Accept God as good? Listen to His voice? Your openness to the support of others around you?

5. Read Psalm 88: 2-3. What is filling your soul today? What emotions are flooding your mind and attitude the most these days?

6. Read I Thessalonians 5:18. Some people think that it means we thank God for every circumstance of life. What is the difference between thanking God for everything and thanking Him in everything? How can this verse help us deal with self-pity?

7. Read II Corinthians 10:5. What thoughts have you been dealing with that are destructive and keep you stuck in your grief? What new statements can you say by faith that can lift you upward?

8. Read John 5:1-9. Share what it would look like if Jesus were to tell you today to, "pick up your mat and walk?" What would it look like for you to live "unstuck?"

Prayer :

Lord, I don't want to be stuck in my grief and pain anymore. I realize that grief is too big of a force for me but it is not too big for you God. Today, would you help me to identify what is keeping me back from moving forward? Help me to release that which keeps me living in the past and propel me to live in the present and look hopefully toward the future. God I believe you have a plan for me and that plan is not to hurt me but to make me a blessing. I trust you and believe you are bringing me through this journey. In the Name of Jesus Christ! Amen!

Chapter 11 Lessons Learned On The Journey

"If you are kind, people may accuse you of selfish, ulterior motives; be kind anyway. If you are successful, you will win some false friends and true enemies; succeed anyway. If you are honest and frank, people may cheat you; be honest and frank anyway. If you find serenity and happiness, they may be jealous; be happy anyway. The good you do today, people will often forget tomorrow; do good anyway...You see, in the final analysis, it is between you and God; it was never between you and them anyway." - Mother Teresa

"**Sometimes**, God puts you down so you can learn how to stand again after a fall." – Adrian Rayshawn

"Keeping our focus on the end goal helps us endure suffering. If we focus on the pain, we can easily lose hope and fall into despair. People today have been so weighed down that it is only natural that a culture of despair has developed. Suffering surfaces what kind of hope we have. We do have hope in this life--but that's not all. Hope in Christ stands in stark contrast to the paralysis or passiveness that would rather lie down and die. Because Christ is victorious over sin and death, that victory is ours as believers. But it is up to us whether we will live in the victory of Christ or instead harden our hearts." -Thomas Finch

The teacher cleared her voice and spoke to the class, *"Listen up, boys and girls, get out your pen and paper and take notes from our lesson today. Tomorrow we have a test."* I think most of us can remember those words. "Take notes!" And then the word, "test" captured our hearts and turned our blood ice cold. We had a test coming. We were very careful to take good notes because we knew there would be a test, and that meant accountability. We realized the better notes we took usually meant the better the grade we were going to get in the class. If you didn't take good notes or if you were daydreaming in class then you were going to face an uncertain future.

What is true in high school and college is also true in the adult real world. It is important all through life to be taking notes. Even if those notes are mental notes. The wisest man who ever lived spoke these words. In Proverbs 9:9, he said, *"Instruct a wise man and he will be wiser still; teach a righteous man and he will add to his learning."*

157

Solomon is saying that if you are observant you will apply what you learn. If you are not observant then you will be destined to repeat the mistakes of life over and over again. Wise people become wise because they apply what they are learning.

They even go another step and actually teach what they are learning to another generation. Scripture tells us that one of the signs of a godly leader in the church is the ability to teach. Inherent in the ability to teach is the ability to learn. You're always a learner before you're a teacher. Teachers teach what they've learned not out of what they don't know. There is nothing as boring as listening to a teacher who doesn't know what they are teaching or is teaching what they fail to practice.

Some of the smartest people I know did not do exceptional in high school. My father was forced to drop out of school at the eighth grade level. But I have never met a man more hungry for learning than my father. Dad is an avid reader and keeps his mind open to learn new truths even into his eighties. Likewise, some of the dumbest people I know have an academic education with certifications on the wall but have not learned to apply it in real life. You may score high on the IQ tests but it is possible that you are flunking in life. God wants us to learn and apply truth accurately. The Bible says that wisdom is the application of truth. And application means we are able to do life successfully. We are applying truth to decisions, relationships, marriage, finances, family, and all of life.

Here's what Solomon, the wisest man who ever lived, said about wisdom. He is the son of the greatest King of Israel that ever lived – David. No doubt he learned from the knee of his father David. Perhaps he learned his wisdom from observing life and what was happening around him. Solomon said,

Ecclesiastes 7:4, *"Yes, a wise man thinks much of death, while the fool thinks only of having a good time now."* And in Proverbs it says, *"I applied my heart to what I observed and I learned a lesson from what I saw."*

Solomon said that during times of death it is a time to think, ponder, and be instructed. On the contrary a fool goes on about life never thinking about eternity. So let me reflect back on my personal journey and share a few points of wisdom that I learned along the way.

1. Suffering is a normal part of life. Look around you! This world is filled with pain, suffering, and heartbreak. Brokenness is part of the human experience. Whether it is cancer, accidents, divorce, or death, brokenness is part of life.

You and I are not the only one suffering. People are dying of cancer, heart problems, and even the simple flu every day. None of us ever consider that death might come knocking on our door and when it does come we feel shocked that we are victims. John 16:33, *"I have told you these things, so that in me you may have peace. In this world you will have trouble."*

One of those days during the recovery phase I took Shelley to *The Shepherd Center* for outpatient observation. I was overcome with a sense of self-pity for what Shelley and I were enduring. When we walked into the waiting room it was filled with young men and women with traumatic brain injuries. Many were being brought in to see their doctor on stretchers, in wheel chairs, and most in very severe conditions. It was as if God spoke to me audibly, "Dan, you think you are dealing with a terrible tragedy, look around you." I looked and my self-pity started to fade. No matter what we are dealing with in life there are others around us that are dealing with much more horrible life experiences. God broke through to me and gave perspective that day!

2. In a moment life can change forever. We are moving along in life and everything is in the normal gear. But then suddenly life can change drastically. We tend to see life as a gradual and progressive movement from one step to another. We move from infancy, to childhood, to elementary school, to high school, to college, to marriage, to our first job, starting a family, the maturing years, nest free years, and on into retirement. We plan our life like we would write the script of a novel or a movie. But God does not guarantee us consistency nor does he guarantee us that our life script will be written the way we like it. Some things in our lives give us no warning. It comes at us unknowingly, like a thief in the night.

Life can lull us into expecting it to continue the same way it was yesterday. But in a moment everything can change forever. James says, "Life is like a vapor it appears for a little time and then vanishes away." We never have the guarantee of another day or year. So, relish today, celebrate today, thank God for today, and enjoy the moments of life because it can and will change.

3. We can't control life or the consequences. We are more out of control on planet earth than we imagine. We pretend that we have it all together but we don't. Most of us are living in a state of denial. Our self-sufficiency lulls us into thinking we can prepare for hurricanes, car crashes, and stock market tumbles. We purchase health, auto, and home insurance to protect us from life's inevitable crises. Society offers us insurance on every household appliance we purchase. Relax and repeat after me, *"I know I live in a world filled with trouble. One day it will happen to me. But until then I will continue to be sufficient in Christ and live in His power."* Let me remind you that life is filled with trouble. Trouble has either come your way, you are in the middle of trouble, or you are just saying goodbye to trouble. Jesus gave wonderful advice in John 16:33, *"I have told you these things, so that in me you may have peace. In this world you will have trouble. But take heart! I have overcome the world."*

4. Don't waste your pain. We can waste our pain if we are not keen journey observers. If we are not careful we will miss the voice of God in our pain. We may even repeat our mistakes over and over again in life. I have seen people go from one bad marriage to another. They repeat that cycle again and again. Solomon would say to us, "Listen and learn." What is God trying to say to you? God never wastes our sorrows!

Our pain can make us bitter and cynical toward life. Our pain can detach us from others around us. Or, our pain can point us toward a path of blessing and help to others.

Look to see how God might actually use your pain to be a blessing to another person. A few months ago a dear friend of mine called me one evening and said, *"Dan, I'm counseling a man who lost his wife and I can't help him and I told him your story. His name is Steve, here he is on the phone."* It was that short of a conversation! I sat and talked to Steve for about 30 minutes while another group was waiting for me to speak in the next room. But God allowed my pain to be of help to this dear fellow traveler in grief. When I finished the listening and question time he said, *"I haven't talked to anyone who knew what I was feeling until I talked to you tonight."* This was not a salute to my brilliance or counseling ability but a reflection on my painful journey. I knew some of what he was feeling and I knew firsthand what it felt like to lose a spouse whom you deeply love.

Let me confess a few things. I look back over my life and realize how insensitive I have been to those dealing with grief. It was not until I suffered the loss of my wife that I knew how much they must have been hurting. Many times I cajoled them for not rising above the pain rather than empathizing with their loss. God will heal our hurt of grief quicker if we can start sharing the story of God's grace and our healing with others.

5. From a pinnacle to the pit is closer than imagined. Three weeks before the accident both Shelley and I had given God praise for his blessing and favor. We were riding God's wave of blessing. In a second, we went from the pinnacle to the pit. Everything in our life went from control to out of control and from order to chaos. It all happened so fast!

Almost every day of the week I hear of people who go from the pinnacle to the pit. They have a good job, they have dual income, they have a beautiful home, and suddenly life takes an unfortunate turn. People lose their job, families lose the extra income, and even the rich have homes that are foreclosed. Suddenly life is a world spinning out of orbit.

One of our deepest needs is for security. None of us want to live a life where security disappears. Every day we seek to hide our fear or insecurity with investments, stocks, bonds, and material security. We long to be prepped for the unexpected pit falls in life. We live with the desire that we have enough money in savings to protect us from the unknown. Isaiah the prophet reminds us, *"You (God) will keep in perfect peace him (or her) whose mind is steadfast, because he (or she) trusts in you. (26:3)"*

6. The things that matter the most in life is the eternal. Almost daily I would write on CaringBridge, and I would ask people to pray for our journey. I realized how important prayer was during this journey. I also realized how important the eternal impact was on so many people's lives. Even today there are people who will stop me and tell me how our journey impacted their life for good.

As I look back over this journey, I can see lives that had been changed and people who been saved. It's the eternal things that really matter in life. Although Satan may have meant it for evil God used it for His good.

When a man or woman comes down to the end of their life they do not think about their bank account. They do not think about buildings, houses, or land. In those final hours we think about important things that will last forever; family, friends, and relationships. We will naturally think of eternal things. No one ever came down to the end of their life and said, *"I really wished I had spent more time at the office!"*

When we gathered around Shelley's side in those last days we had the assurance that for Shelley to be, "absent from the body was to be present with the Lord." No material wealth can give one that assurance as a living faith in Christ. Eternity issues matter the most.

7. You have never had your faith tested until you face a crisis so big that it lays you flat on your back. Faith by definition is something that needs to be tested to be proven. I thought I knew what crises and testing was all about. But I did not have a clue until grief hit me. Most of us feel fairly confident that we are prepared for the unexpected winds of adversity. But when life hits hard it will knock us off our feet. Money can't bail us out and the medical community has given up hope. This is where real faith is tested. So it is in the crucible of life that we find out what we are made out of, whether what we have been taught is true, and whether God really is all sufficient.

I remember sitting with a friend as he was pondering the pain of personal family crisis. Here was a man who taught the Bible to others almost every week. He had counseled beside the bed of friends who faced enormous life crisis. He had spoken the words of faith, confidence, and assurance to others. Now he was facing his own personal crisis. And he simply sat across the table and cried out, "Why God?" It was a Job moment in his life. If you have never said it, I know you have thought it, "Why God?" None of us can understand why some things happen. We are just told to trust. Proverbs 3; 5-6 says, *"Trust in the Lord with all your heart lean not unto your own understanding in all your ways acknowledge him and he will direct your path."* Sometimes all you can do is simply trust God when you cannot understand him.

During this journey I cried out so many times, "Why God?" I did not understand why others had suffered a similar accident and ended up walking away. I wondered why God had not chosen to take Shelley and me both home on the day of the accident; it seemed so much cleaner! I wondered why God allowed so many set backs on the journey and only a few steps forward. And, I often cried out in pain, "Why God?" And too many times there was silence. I was left to wonder, ponder, cry, and trust. To this day I still don't understand many of the twists and turns of our journey. Many things don't make sense. But I am simply left to trust. Whom else do we turn if we walk away from God?

8. Some the greatest tests come in our interpretation of the scriptures. I have preached the Bible for over thirty years. I have had to counsel people who have lost a loved one due to death. I have counseled young couples suffering the loss of their only child. However, I have never had to wrestle with the Biblical ramification of grief until someone close to me died. Then everything you believe about God and the Bible is tested. Someone humorously said, *"The difference between major surgery and minor surgery is whether you are undergoing the surgery or me."* True!

I can tell you personally, that contrary to what I had originally thought, hearing scripture quoted to you is not always helpful. I had many friends who would quote scripture to remind me of God's promises. I had put many of those scriptures to memory over the years so they were very dear to my heart. But when people quoted those scriptures to me it caused me greater frustration than help. I know this may seem contrary to what I had always believed about ministry in crisis and grief.

People tossing out scripture sometimes seemed like iodine to my open wound. I just wanted someone to sit with me and listen to my pain. I wanted God with skin on! I felt like I was in triage and they wanted to rush me into rehab. One man told me he just wished someone would simply hug him like his wife used to hug him. There is something about grief that makes idle words, trite solutions, and scripture quotes less than a solace.

One of the greatest challenges happened within a week of the funeral. I sat back and began to think about heaven and the reality that one day Shelley and I would see each other again. Everything would be made right and whole in heaven. Then, it hit me like a jolt of lightening. The scriptures tell us that there is no marriage in heaven.

Luke 20:34-36, Jesus replied, *"The people of this age marry and are given in marriage But those who are considered worthy of taking part in that age and in the resurrection from the dead will neither marry nor be given in marriage."* And in Matt 22:29-31 it says, *"At the resurrection people will neither marry nor are given in marriage."*

Those words cause agony and another faith stretch for weeks. I had lost my wife forever. I now understood why the Mormon doctrine of the eternal family is so enticing. To think that I would be in heaven without Shelley as my wife was more than I could imagine. I loved Shelley and the relationship of husband and wife almost as much as I loved God. My faith was sent in a tailspin. I was struggling and in inner turmoil!

Then, as I began to ponder those Scriptures, I realized that Jesus compared the glories of heaven to the commonness of earth. On earth, things are good, but God describes heaven as so much better. Revelation 21:3-4 describes heaven, *"He will wipe every tear from their eyes. There will be no more death or mourning or crying or pain, for the old order of things has passed away."*

In heaven the Bible describes it as a place with golden bricks for streets, pearls for doors, and mansions for houses. In heaven all the former things are gone and everything is new. In heaven everything is far better. It was like a light turned on!

So, if I believe that everything in heaven is better, I eventually concluded that the relationship of marriage, although very beautiful on earth, would be far greater in heaven. So, I won the battle theologically in my mind and heart. Heaven was going to be far better than anything on earth and the marriage relationship on earth would pale to the relationship we would have together in heaven. I still don't understand the full dimensions of that new relationship, but at the heart of the gospel it teaches, it will be far better. Another lesson learned about trusting in the heart of God!

9. Hold on to what you have always known true about God. For me there were nights and days of weeping, crying, complaining, and brokenness. I apologize for the lack of faith that I showed during these times. I was in deep internal struggle with my view of God, blessings, and His will that left me struggling alone. In spite of all the prayer, Shelley was left disabled mentally, emotionally, and physically due to the traumatic brain injury. Then, at her death I was left totally alone.

I remember nights looking up to the heavens begging God to answer prayer. He had done it for others and I knew he could do it for me. Why didn't God just simply raise Shelley out of her coma? Why didn't God help her to come out of her coma quicker? When she did awaken I asked God why did it take so long for rehabilitated. After her death why did God choose *that* ending to her life? I must admit I was angry! I had served God so faithfully and I had sacrificed for him. After all, I was a minister of the gospel. Didn't I deserve to get *my* miracle?

I want you to know what I learned in this journey. God is big enough to handle your anger, your hostility, and your most passionate cries. When you go through an unexplainable crisis it will test your faith. You cannot allow your view of God to be warped by the present but you must hold on to what you have always known about God. In the past, before the crisis, you knew God to be compassionate, loving, kind, and always wanting His best for your life. Grief has clouded your view of God's character and jaded your faith. So cry out and tell Him everything. Tell Him your hurts, pains, and your suffering. He is big enough to hear your words, feel your anger, and still love you. Some of those times I believe I could hear the sobs of Jesus crying with me at the death of Shelley. If he did it for Lazarus I'm sure he would have cried for Shelley.

10. There are some things worse than death. I remember many nights crying out to God and saying something like this, "Lord, I wish it were me. I wish I was the one in the coma. I wish I was the one suffering. I wish I was in that grave." Sometimes living is harder than dying. It's harder to live through a crisis journey when the one you love has been taken from you. It's as if your soul has been ripped in two. That was which was joined at marriage, has now been ripped apart. You are a different person and you are no longer the same as you were when you were married.

I have heard people counseled in tragedy, *"Take heart, you ought to be so thankful you are alive."* Before you say those words remember you don't understand what the person is going through. They wished they could have died as well. They feel like life is over for them, and in a true sense, the past is over. The former life is behind them. That loved one cannot come back. So we must deal with the unknown and the change that the crisis is brought in our life. Believe me when I say, "there are some things worse than death." The thing that is worse than death is to go on living after the death of your spouse or loved one.

11. **Crisis will reveal your real friends**. Crisis has a way of bringing out the best and the worst in people. God sends angels of mercy from unexpected sources. On this journey God sent a medical doctor that lived three houses down who volunteered his services. God sent several nurses who came to visit Shelley and helped us in our moments of greatest despair. God sent pastoral friends who visited the hospital, prayed, encouraged, and believed with us. God sent people who gave up their vacation to come and help us build the upstairs apartment for mom and dad. God moved the hearts of ladies from the radiology department at Honey Creek who dropped off forty dollars collected from the nurses after our visit. God moved the hearts of thousands who sent cards, phone calls, and emails. They just reminded us that we were not alone and we had a family of faith who were there to support us.

And then there were those who made bold promises to be there but never showed up. I believe they meant well. I think some people over promised out of pity but when reality hit they did not have the energy, strength, or resources. So, you just move on and thank God for every little blessing. You can believe the best in people or the worst in people. I have tried to believe the best and move ahead. But you do learn who your comforters and comrades are when you go through a crisis!

12. **When the test doesn't fit - God whittles away at you to make you fit the test.** I have never enjoyed visiting hospitals. Even as a pastor hospital visits were not my favorite calling. If I could, I would defer hospital visitation to my pastoral staff. There are some people that have the gift of chaplaincy; but not me. They love to nurture people in crisis. They are thrilled by a visit to an emergency ward. I confess, that is not my gifting.

I believe I could have handled Shelley's death at the time of the accident much easier than her coma, mental deformity, and her rehabilitation. Can you imagine three months in a coma? And then she awoke with atrophy, with mental deficiency, with an inability to care for herself, and that was the best prognosis. There were so many questions about her future and mine. I thought to myself many times, *"Lord, this is more than I can handle. My test does not conform to my personality!"*

During the two and a half years of Shelley's life, I was up early. I did the dishes, washed clothes, fixed our meals, provided medicine, and served as my wife's caregiver. Shelley, had always been my, "caregiver." She's the one who washed, made the bed, did the dishes, prepared the taxes, and did a thousand other chores around the house. Now, I was doing both hers and mine. I felt like David in Saul's armor! The test did not fit my personality. So, God would fit me for the test. He prodded me and pushed me. He forced me into a role that I would never have chosen for myself.

Apostle Paul said this on his journey in II Corinthians 12:7 – 10, *"to keep me from becoming conceited because of these surpassingly great revelations, there was given the authority my flesh, a messenger of Satan, to torment me. Three times I pleaded with the Lord to take it away from me. But he said to me, "my grace is sufficient for you, for my power is made perfect in weakness." Therefore I will boast all the more gladly about my weaknesses, so that Christ's power may rest on me. That is why, for Christ's sake, I delight in weaknesses, and insults, and hardships, in persecutions, in difficulties. For when I'm weak, then I'm strong."*

The Living Bible says it this way, *"no, but I am **with you**; that is all you need. My power shows up best in weak people."* So it was about God getting glory through my life. It was not about me having a test that fits my personality or my gifting. It was about radical inner surgery. It was about God shaping me for the test in spite of my personality.

13. **When everything slips away you can count on God.** There is a great passage in Proverbs 18:24 that says, *"...there is a friend that sticks closer than a brother."* We all need someone when we go through crisis; a brother, a father, a friend. Thank God He has promised to be all of those and more. We are not alone no matter what we feel like. God is in the midst of your suffering and struggle even if you don't see Him or feel Him!

What are the things that really matter in life? It is salvation, and knowing that you have a home in heaven. It is not a dependency on doctors, medicine, insurances, or any temporal dependency. When all else has failed you still have God. Hannah Whitehall Smith in her great devotional book said it best, *"God is enough."* In Joshua 1:5, God said to Joshua, *"As I was with Moses, so I will be with you; I will never leave you nor forsake you."* He is steadfast and immovable in his love and compassion for us.

John Wesley died on Wednesday March 2, 1791, in his eighty-eighth year. As he lay dying, his friends gathered around him, Wesley grasped their hands and said repeatedly, "Farewell, farewell." At the end, summoning all his remaining strength, he cried out, *"The best of all is, God is with us,"* lifted his arms and raised his feeble voice again, repeating the words, **"The best of all is, God is with us."**

You do not have to go through what Shelley and I had to endure to hear God's voice and learn the vital lessons of life. You do not have to experience pain and tragedy to learn lessons that will save you from hardship in difficulty.

As you read this you may have sensed that God is speaking to you today. You have lived the blessed life, you have experienced good days and blessed days beyond what you deserve. What lesson in this list is God speaking to you about?

In Hebrews 3:15, it says, *"Today, if you hear God's voice speaking to you, do not harden your heart against him."* Maybe God is calling your name in the middle of your pain and welcoming you to enter into a new relationship of forgiveness and healing.

No matter how long you've ignored God and his voices. He still loves you and he still wants to have a relationship with you. God is trying to get your attention. He is calling you to a new and different life. And best of all He is with you.

So I conclude this chapter with this prayer that I invite you to pray. *"Jesus Christ, I understand that you want a relationship with me. I want to get to know you and hear your voice. Help me to be more open to impressions that you want to give me. Help me to see how even pain can bring me closer to you. Today, Jesus Christ, I want to open up my life, ask you to forgive my sin, and forgive my lack of trust. I accept you as my Lord and Savior. Today I give you the keys of my life. Be the manager of my life and lead me and guide me and save me."*

If you prayed that prayer and meant it from your heart then you have started a new relationship with Jesus Christ. Your sins have been forgiven. You have a new relationship, and the first thing you need to do is to tell someone. Tell the closest person to you. Tell them that today you stepped across a line and made Jesus Christ your Savior.

If you have been serving Christ but have wandered away, then pray and ask Jesus to once again take control of your life. Offer Him anew the keys to your life and future. Let Him heal your pain and provide you with power to face another day.

CHAPTER ELEVEN STUDY GUIDE:

1. Discussion: Describe a time in your life when the teacher said, "It is test time!"   What were your emotions like when the teacher gave the announcement? Describe several reasons that people don't always do well when they have a, "surprise test?" Usually the teacher stays quiet during test time!

2. Read Proverbs 9:9 and discuss the difference between intellect and wisdom?

3. Read Ecclesiastes 7:4, and share one of the key lessons you have learned about life and death in general. Why should a wise person consider eternity and death?

4. Read the list of 10 lessons the author states that he learned during his journey.   Which one of the 10 lessons is the most beneficial to you personally today?

5. Have you ever felt that your "test" did not fit you or your personality? How is God shaping you today to make you fit the test instead of changing the test?

6. In Joshua 1:5, there is a promise that God gave Joshua and it is ours as well. What encouragement does it give you to know that God will never leave you or forsake you? Have there been times when you felt like God had left or forsaken you? What is the difference between feeling forsaken and being forsaken?

7. As a group, quietly pray the final prayer together. If you desire to talk to someone about your spiritual life or the need to make a decision to trust Jesus, do so as soon as possible.

Prayer

Lord, I recognize that I am a student enrolled in the school of faith. You are instructing me in new insights daily. Help me to open up my eyes and my life to your lessons. Help me to trust your heart when I cannot see your hand. Help me to lean on your Word daily for strength and hope. I give you permission to use the testing times of my trial to forge me into a deeper and more devoted follower of Jesus. In the Name of Jesus! Amen

171

12 No More Cloudy Days

Isa 43:19 "See, I am doing a new thing ! Now it springs up; do you not perceive it? I am making a way in the desert and streams in the wasteland." NIV

"I believe in second chances, I believe in angels, too, I believe in new romances Baby, I believe in you, These cloudy days are coming to an end, And you don't have to be afraid to fall in love again." – Glenn Lewis Frey – The Eagles

"Though no one can go back and make a brand new start, anyone can start from now and make a brand new ending." -Unknown

"The most incredible thing about miracles is that they happen." G.K. Chesterton

Over the past few years the travel industry has been in the news. The cruise lines have especially made the front page. Each week thousands of people board a huge ocean liner and head toward the promises of open seas and vacation bliss. Many have invested their savings to find some sense of peace, tranquility, and relaxation. But instead some have found their vacation vessel adrift at sea without electricity, running water, and food. Their vacation paradise has turned into a nightmare.

There is a song that we sung as children that says, *"Oh, give me a home…. Where seldom is heard a discouraging word. And the skies are not cloudy all day."* Everyone envisions a Shangri-La of unclouded happiness; no more disappointments, cancer, disease, and nightmares. We are looking for those uncloudy days. But, as the story of life goes, right in the middle of paradise something tragic happens.

Over the past pages you have read the story of our accident, hospitalization, fight for rehabilitation, and eventually the death of my wife Shelley. The weeks and months afterward were filled with grief and pain that broke my spirit. Gradually, over time, you begin to heal and think about the future. My process of healing involved a litany of self-directed questions. Dan, do you want to move ahead or live in the past? Dan, will grief define your life? Dan, do you want to live alone or get married again?

Several months after the death of my wife I sat down in an O'Charleys Restaurant in Snellville, GA with a friend and his wife. At the end of the meal they said that they had been praying for me and they both had arrived at the same conclusion; I needed a spouse and they had a good recommendation.

Over the previous months I could feel the intensity building from my friends. Several of them were on the "prowl" to solve my loneliness problem. Although I could not see myself getting married again the conversation sparked my curiosity. I thought, "Who do they see fits my personality?" So, I left that evening and went home to check out their recommendation on Facebook. Yes, Facebook! I have always been very suspicious of internet connections but this was different . . . it was a recommendation from a dear friend and I was curios. When I opened her page I saw something in her eyes; the pain. I believe the grief pain in her eyes attracted me first. So, here begins another chapter in this unfolding story of cloudy and uncloudy days!

As Paul Harvey use to say, "Now for the rest of the story!" to this traumatic journey. So, I have asked, that girl with the pain in her eyes, Debbie Braisted to share her story in her own words.

On Thursday, September 10, 2009, we were heading home after picking up yard sale items. We had just dropped them by the church for our annual mission's yard sale. While we sat at the stop light my husband Joe said he wanted to run by Lowe's to look at something. He had been working on our home shower and wanted to ask a few questions about proper installation of a shower in our laundry room.

It was also a time of expectation and joy. In two weeks, our oldest son, daughter-in-law, and grandson were coming home from the mission field to spend four months with us. They are missionaries in the Dominican Republic. They were coming home to prepare for the birth of our second grandchild in November. She would be the first girl in the Paul Braisted generation and we were so excited. Joe looked at me and asked if I wanted him to take me home before he drove the mile to Lowes. My reply was a statement I have heard echo over the past years, "No, I'll go with you. I just want to be with you." The light turned green and the car sped up as we headed toward Lowes.

We only made it about a hundred yards when I noticed the van slowing down. Joe turned to me and said, "Debbie you better......." It was all that quick and sudden. Joe slumped over the steering wheel and I quickly, almost mechanically, took the steering wheel as his hands fell to his side.

I unbuckled my seatbelt and slid out of the passenger seat to stop the van. The car was moving fairly slow by now. I put the car in park and pushed Joe back against the seat. I realized the seriousness of the moment and I began to cry. I was both crying and praying all at the same time. This was crisis time like I had never experienced!

Like an angel from heaven, a lady showed up beside the passenger window to help. Somehow, I knew she was a nurse. I was weeping as I cried out, "Someone help me, call 911." I was praying with all my strength that this was not really happening and once we got Joe help at the hospital everything would be fine. I looked into Joe's face and his eyes were open at first. Then, in what seemed like only a minute, he began to make snoring sounds and his eyes closed. He made two more sounds and his body went lifeless.

By now my son Joshua, who was only a few blocks away,

was at my side. My son later told me that he knew those sounds were his last breath leaving his body. The lady informed me she was a nurse. They hurried to get Joe out on the street. Then they begin CPR while we waited for the EMT to arrive.

During those moments of pain I knew there were angels all around. I watched in wonder as Joe laid on the street not breathing. People came up to comfort me and would then disappear into the crowd and others step forward. I looked down the busy street, three lanes on each side, and there was a human barricade that formed to block his body from the traffic.

By the time the EMT's had arrived and begin to work on him we knew it was over. Joe was coded dead before we even arrived to the hospital. I knew in my heart he was gone. I saw his sweet spirit leave his body immediately. But I just kept praying and hoping, "Please God, bring him back to me!" I begged God to change His mind and perform a miracle of miracles all for His glory. But it was not to be!

One moment, just a second, and my life was turned upside down. I needed Joe. I didn't know what to do without him! We did everything together for the past twenty-eight years. I hurt deep down inside! For me grief was more than an emotional hurt, it was actually physically painful. The life that I knew had ended that day and was over forever.

I lived for months thinking back over what life was like before. Joe was a wonderful, godly man, a wonder-ful husband, my best friend, my partner in everything. He loved his children (Michael, Joshua, and Timothy) and our grandson Landon was the apple of his eye. He couldn't wait to hold his granddaughter in November. Joe knew how to relate to all ages and he loved people. Everywhere we lived and worked Joe left a lasting posi-tive impression. He struggled in feeling like he was never able to do enough for the Church and God's people. I am convinced that God rewarded my Joe by taking him home. His life was short but he gave his very best in following the Lord.

I went through months and months of anguish, grief and pain. Looking back I must have been pitiful to live with. Most of the time I would gather just enough energy needed to go to work and do my job. Then I would come home and collapse. Everything was dependent upon my salary, my energy, and my decisions.

Before, my salary was for the extras, and now my salary had to cover everything. Someone introduced me to a Presbyterian Church in town that needed a Worship Director and that gave me a second job. I was still just paying the bills and living a strained life. I was praying that God would give me a reason for living again!

I had always found my identity beside my husband. He was the main breadwinner. He was the pastor. I loved being a pastor's wife and of course working with the music. I thought to myself many times, "Where do I fit in now?" I still felt like a pastor's wife inside. But now it was so hard to return back to the church in which we had ministered together.

One Sunday I returned to our home church. A lady was sitting behind me and she appeared to be a visitor. She asked, "Are you the wife of the pastor who died?" She said she had come back to visit the church because of our ministry. I told another parishioner about the lady to help her get better connected and the lady said, "Debbie, that is no longer your concern!" People mean well but can say the stupidest things. I'm hoping it was a comment meant to ease my worries but it drove in the point that my former life was over..

Now what? I just wanted to crawl in bed to sleep the rest of my life away. My boys had seemingly gone on with their lives. They miss their dad but my life was their dad. I was living life in survival mode. I worked two jobs and came home to my lonely life. I tried to *serve the Lord and help others anyway I could. After all, I had accepted that this was God's plan for my life. I had to trust Him.*

One lonely evening, I was checking my Facebook account and I had a message from Dan Berry. Joe and I were acquainted with Shelley and Dan from years back serving in the same district. Our church had been praying for them since the accident and I knew Shelley had died many months ago. Dan sent a short note asking how I was coping with Joe's death and that he was praying for me. I responded that it was difficult and I was praying for him also. And so began our communications. Every day or two we would send a short message; sharing how we were dealing with our grief. He was attending Grief-Share so he shared about the sessions weekly. I began to look forward to those notes and the communication started coming more frequent. It was so nice to talk with someone that knew what I was going through. The old saying is true, "Misery loves company."

As we talked and shared our stories, we could see how God had woven our lives together; churches, districts, friends, likes, dislikes, music, food, but most of all our desire to serve God with our broken lives. It all started off as a good friendship. But through those conversations, healing began. Joy started to invade my heart again. After many emails and phone calls, Dan and I started the long drives to spend time with each other. Wouldn't you know, my sister Beverly happened to live in Atlanta. It made it all very convenient. Dating is not fun at our age, but being alone is even worst. We were too old to start over again and too young to be alone. So we started taking small steps forward to see if this was where God was leading us.

There are so many things in relationships to consider when you are thinking of starting a new and different life together. Our God, our boys, and our family were our first priority. Dan and I talked and asked so many ques-

tions. Let me rephrase that; Dan asked so many questions. I guess maybe a million or so! At least it seemed
that way. We laugh because my answers are short and
to the point and Dan, well, he pontificates. But really at
this stage in our lives we had to know as much as possible
and as quickly as possible. Dan and Shelley had a great
marriage and Joe and I had a great marriage. After all
the questions and answers, we wanted a great marriage
the second time; more than just a good friendship! We
wanted another God blessed marriage.
On July 17, 2011 we were married. Jason, Dan's first son
is pastor at the 12Stone Church in Flowery Branch, and
he performed the wedding. All five boys were present for
the event. When it came time to have the groom kiss the
bride Jason lightened up the moment by saying, "Dad, for
the good of your boys up on the stage. Please briefly and
respectfully kiss your bride."
Oh don't get me wrong, the pain of losing Joe and our
life together was still there. It will always be there. But
this is also one of the many blessings God has given Dan
and me. Our boys say we are strange because we share
so much of our past marriages together. I cry when Dan
is hit with the pain of Shelley's death and Dan cries with
me when I get hit with the pain of Joe's death. This is our
life and we are so blessed to have each other.
God has also given me a ministry again. I travel with
Dan every weekend to one of the almost forty churches
on the district. We have a great marriage that I never
knew I could have again. He preaches and teaches, and I
sing and play the piano again. I could never have imagined that God had another chapter of ministry for my
life.

Can you imagine that God could take two broken, bruised,
and hurting people and bring them happiness again? Debbie and I
are blessed to have each other at this stage of our life. Each day the
clouds are lifting and we are more and more seeing God's handi-

work. Together we stand as a testimony of God's grace and mercy. I like to tell her that "misery loves company" and I am the misery and she is the company. I tell you that God is good and He is faithful in spite of all of our past hurts and pains. He has a plan for our broken lives and I thank God for His gracious gift of Debbie. God did not promise us an easy life. He did not promise us that there would be no trouble but He did promise to be faithful until the end. Like the three Hebrew children, he promised He would be with us IN the fire and I assure you He will be with you in you're the middle of those hottest flames of adversity and trial. He is faithful!

If you have lost a loved one, Debbie and I know a little about that grief. Yes, there are many cloudy days after the death of a loved one. The journey is not easy but there is hope. Best of all there is hope beyond this life into the next one called heaven.

God has put a longing in our hearts for heaven. So many people try to avoid the conversation about eternity until life begins to end. Let me assure you that Jesus believed in heaven. Jesus taught that it was a real place with real people just like you and me. Intuitively, God has put something within us that cries out, "*There must be more than this!*" Peggy Lee wrote a song that says, "*Is that all there is, is that all there is. If that's all there is my friends, then let's keep dancing. Let's break out the booze and have a ball. If that's all there is.*" But there is more!

Something inside us witnesses to the claim that there is more than planet earth. We cannot help but look upward! Deep down inside of every person there is the silent witness that there IS more to life than cruise ships, tropical vacations, another home at the lake, and more cash in the bank. We know instinctively that there just has to be more – way more! We are nostalgic for what we have never seen but only know intuitively in our hearts.

> Can you hear the sighing in the wind? Can you feel the heavy silence in the mountains? Can you sense the restless longing in the sea? Can you see it in the woeful eyes of an animal? Something's coming. . . something better."
> – Joni Eareckson Tada

The Bible describes a day on planet earth when everything was perfect. Adam and Eve were in the garden and all of God's

creation was in harmony. Then through the act of disobedience
sin came into the world. Our human nature was stained by sin and
Eden was lost. The perfect paradise was lost and our world has
become corrupt by continued disobedience and sin. Revelation
21:1-5 vividly describes this new Eden.

*"Then I saw a new heaven and a new earth, for the first
heaven and the first earth had passed away, and there was no longer
any sea. I saw the Holy City, the new Jerusalem, coming down out
of heaven from God, prepared as a bride beautifully dressed for her
husband. And I heard a loud voice from the throne saying, "Now the
dwelling of God is with men, and he will live with them. They will
be his people, and God himself will be with them and be their God.
He will wipe every tear from their eyes. There will be no more death
or mourning or crying or pain, for the old order of things has passed
away. He who was seated on the throne said, "I am making everything new!"* NIV

This is our eternal home - heaven. When we get to heaven
it shall be the climax of the ages. It is the fulfillment of our every
prayer. Heaven is the end of the journey for ultimate fulfillment,
joy, and eternal happiness. Best of all, there shall be no more funer-
als or grief counseling there. Just imagine! What a place!
Heaven is like nothing we know down here on planet earth. In
heaven there are no flaws, recalls, or defaults; only perfection. In
heaven every friendship and relationship will be better than anything we have known down on earth. In heaven we shall see our
loved ones who have exited planet earth with a faith in Christ. Best
of all we shall see Jesus face to face. When we see Him we will see
that our loved ones have been safely in the hands of our Savior.
Together we will be safe in heaven forever!

It takes faith both to believe or not to believe in heaven.
If you are a believer in Jesus then you have taken the step of faith to
believe the Bible and make the faith jump. Otherwise, you are still
trying to make up your mind. Let me recommend you walk down
the aisle of the book department at your nearest Wal-Mart or Target

department store. You will find many titles that try to prove the existence of heaven and the afterlife. You will find writers like Dr. Eben Alexander in her book called, "Proof of Heaven," who makes a case for heaven from a medical doctor's perspective. While in a coma Dr. Alexander experienced a journey beyond this world and encountered a super-physical existence. She came out of her experience convinced that there is a real soul and that death is not the end of personal existence.

Recently the book, Heaven Is for Real is the story of a four-year old son of a small town Nebraska pastor who experienced heaven during emergency surgery. He talked about looking down to see the doctor operating and his dad praying in the waiting room. The family didn't know what to believe but soon the evidence was clear. In heaven, Colton met his miscarried sister whom no one ever had told him about and his great-grandfather who died 30 years before Colton was born. He shared impossible-to-know details about each.

There are many claims about seeing heaven; some are believable but others are actually contradictory to scripture. Ultimately you have to decide biblically whether you believe that God's promises all through scripture are true. Stories can inspire but the Bible is our authority. Do you believe Jesus when he said, *"In my Father's house are many mansions. . . I go to prepare a place for you."*(John 14:1-2)

God has provided a way for us all to join Him in Heaven. In the middle of our joys, pain, anticipation, and suffering on earth God has provided a way out. It is more than wishful thinking, but an authentic path provided by the grace of God through Jesus Christ on the cross. We have an anchor in Jesus which provides every one the opportunity to know without a shadow of a doubt that heaven can be ours.

I remember the moment in my life when it happened. I was raised in the church most of my life. When I was five years old we moved from the Berry Farm on the peninsula of Virginia to Baltimore, Maryland. My dad surrendered his life to God and soon afterward gave up the family farm for city life. I feel like singing a verse of, "Green Acres." He was a church planter and we were poor. It is amazing that it is not until later in life that you even realize how poor you were. But we were poor in riches but wealthy in obedience!

Most of my adolescent years I spent in the church and attending camp meeting in Denton, Maryland. I remember going to the altar so many times and then getting back up and returning back to my "old ways." I soon learned to play the part of the hypocrite. I acted one way on the outside, but another way when no one was looking.

Then the day came for me to leave home and head off to college at United Wesleyan College in Allentown, Pennsylvania. I soon ran with the wrong crowd. Someone said, "Water seeks its own source." I told myself I was stretching the wings of freedom, but in all honesty I was in a state of youthful rebellion. It was not a pretty sight!

"Faith is taking the first step even when you don't see the marble staircase." – Martin Luther King, Jr

When God can't get through to you in the natural world He will use the supernatural world. One January afternoon in 1972 I was asleep on my college bed. I had a dream that changed my life. I dreamed that I was lost in the fiery flames of hell and God showed me in a flash where my life was headed without Him. I awoke weeping and in internal turmoil. I felt impelled to surrender my life to Christ like nothing I had ever done before. At the same time I was confessing my sins I was also surrendering my life to serve Him in whatever capacity he desired. Even a willingness to be a missionary!

If you are thinking that somehow you can earn heaven by your good deeds, forget it. I've tried that route and it doesn't get you saving peace. We owe a debt we cannot repay by enough good deeds or kind acts of compassion. But you can, in a moment, realize that you are lost and can do nothing to save yourself. Confess to God your desperation! Then God forgives our sins and gives us a new heart, a mission, and a new destination; heaven. There is a great discourse by Jesus in John 14. He describes heaven and he concludes with this poignant statement; *"I am the way and the truth and the life. No one comes to the Father except through me."* John 14: 6 NIV

One of these days Heaven will be our home. My father is now eighty four years old and we talk just about every day of the week. Dad has reached the stage in life where he feels that his usefulness has passed him by. He increasingly talks more about heaven. I remind him of the importance of his prayers for our family; kids, grandkids, and great grandkids. We need his prayers more than he might imagine.

Last week on the phone I asked him to draw from some of life's lessons over eighty years. Finally I wrestled something out of him. He said, *"Oh, the foolishness of youth."* I asked him to explain his comments. He went on to share that when you are young and healthy you think of retirement and old age as a distant image. You see older people who are facing the age of pains, aches, hospitals, and dementia, but you never imagine it could happen to you. Suddenly you awaken to find you have arrived in the land of the retired and the "has been." Then, with fatherly wisdom he said, *"Dan, whatever you want to do for God and for your family do it today! Life passes by all too quickly."*

"Life passes by all too quickly," are truthful words. Eternity waits for no one. Today is the day to make eternal choices with heavenly consequences. James 4:14 say, *"What is your life? You are a mist that appears for a little while and then vanishes."* NIV So, I want to make the most of everyday of my life.

Whatever trial you are facing just know that God will give you abundant grace for your time of need. James 1:12 say, *"Blessed is the man who perseveres under trial, because when he has stood the test, he will receive the crown of life that God has promised to those who love him." NIV*

Keep pressing forward because God has another chapter for your life. At the depth of our grief we both could never have believed that God had another chapter. For both of us, we had to discover that God wanted us to move forward. We have so much to live for that cannot be seen clearly when travelling the lonely road of grief. We have our kids and our grandkids, and the hope of more grandkids to come! We have a ministry where God is still opening doors. Every week we are engaged in helping others who are going through similar tests. Debbie and I receive phone calls from friends and strangers asking how to get, "unstuck" out of their pit of grief. God has a plan for us! But, good news! God has a plan for you as well! It may not seem like it today, but there is another chapter for your life. *Don't give up! Trust God! He is faithful!*

I can't imagine what you are going through right now. But God knows! You may be going into a crisis, in the middle of a crisis, or coming out of crisis. Take hope, God has a plan for your life. Even when God says, "no," there is hope. He is not finished with you yet. You may never understand all the reasons why the dark clouds have rolled into your life, but I can assure you that God is in control – He is faithful. When you cannot trace His hand you can trust His heart. He will never leave you in your crisis! He will never forsake you! If you lean into God He will bring you through as well.

A few nights ago we had the joy of hearing the Brooklyn Tabernacle Choir. One of their members recently wrote a song that grabbed my heart. It is the story in summary of this book and my life; *"Faithful to the End"*.

When I'm feeling afraid, Full of uncertainty
When the plans that I've made, All fall apart
When the future's unclear, And all that I can do is wait
There is a promise, Echoing in my heart
He will be faithful to the end, He will provide time and time again

185

He will be faithful, So faithful to the end
He will be there when all else fades, His love is stronger than my pain
He will be faithful, So faithful to the end

There is grace I can't measure, Mercy I don't deserve
There's forgiveness that's endless for me, Oh what a blessed assurance
To know how deeply I'm loved, And I'm always reminded
That he will be all I need

I assure you that in the middle of your pain God is there and He is faithful. You may be asking, "Why would God choose me for this trial?" I don't understand the depth of his works but I do trust His heart. And I have found Him faithful through the journey!

Life is filled with both sunny and cloudy days. We all desire to have a life without suffering, separation, setbacks, pain, and death. Jesus said, *"In this world you will have tribulation."* This is not heaven, this is planet earth. The very desire that God has placed for those, "uncloudy days" is God's call to keep our eyes focused on our mission on earth, but also on our eternal home in heaven. It is not until you lose a loved one that you start thinking intensely about the joys and reality of heaven.

Maybe you feel you are at your breaking point today. You can't go on another day. You may feel like you have been beaten down spiritually. Maybe you have failed in some way, shape, or form. Maybe there has been a history of failure and poor decisions in your life and now you are facing the painful consequences.

Maybe you wonder at times why God hasn't just given up on you. But God knows what is happening in your life. He sees your struggles, but He also sees beyond your struggles. . Give your failures and frustrations to Him. Amazingly, God believes in you even when stop believing in yourself! *Trust Him! He is faithful!*

You can't stop those cloudy days from coming, but you can decide your souls direction in the winds of adversity. You can leverage the pain for greater gain. Here is a wonderful thought: *Don't waste your pain.* Use it for greater good and God's glory!

As a teenager I purchased a small sunfish sailboat that needed loving attention and many repairs. After the boat had been repaired I took the boat out on a trial run on the Fenwick Island Bay. It was a fairly windy day but I was young and a sucker for adventure. Without knowing much about sailing I found myself on the boat and pulling on the rigging to tighten the sail. Like a rocket I was out of control, skipping across the waves at a faster speed than I imagined a sail boat might travel. I did say I had never sailed before didn't I? In a few minutes I had traveled out of control into the middle of the bay. Finally, I released the rope on the sail and the boat came to a halt. Now I was left to ponder my situation. I was helpless and adrift!

I remembered my dad's words of wisdom on the beach before I launched, *"Dan, you'll have to tack back and forth to make progress against the wind!"* Tacking is when a sailing vessel turns its bow through the wind so that the direction from which the wind blows changes from one side to the other. It's like going two steps forward and one step back. After about an hour of trial and failure I got the hang of it. Tacking back and forth against the wind I was able to finally get back safely to shore. When you tack you don't make as quick of a journey, but you get there! I remember kissing the sandy beach out of gratitude to have survived the wild ordeal. That was the last time I captained the sailboat and it was one of the best lessons I ever learned about life. *"Dan, you have to tack to make progress against the wind!"*

Those cloudy and windy days of adversity seem overwhelming and forceful for our demise. You may feel like you are sitting helplessly in the middle of the "bay" stuck! But if we can "tack" we can use the winds for God's greater purpose. We don't have to stay adrift or stuck. We don't have to waste our pain but we can actually use our pain, suffering, hurt, and grief to make a positive difference. Just like a judo master uses the weight of the oncoming attacker to his benefit, we can use the weight of grief and leverage it for greater good.

I cannot explain the whys of my journey but I have come to realize that God has a grander purpose in mind than I might imagine. I may never understand the "whys" but I have learned to trust His unfailing love and faithfulness. My pain and suffering has the ear of my heavenly Father! He is greater than death, hell, scars, and grief!

May I lovingly encourage you to leverage the grief for the purpose of blessing those around you? Start today to "tack" against the winds of adversity. Use your pain to make a difference in the people around you. There is no better day to start than today!

CHAPTER TWELVE STUDY GUIDE:
1. Discussion: Describe what you think heaven will be like? Do you sense deep in your heart that there is some mysterious pull toward heaven? What do you think the author means when he said, "Deep down within everyone there is a silent witness?"
2. Read the following verses and describe a picture of heaven from the scriptures. John 14: 1-6; I Cor. 2:9; Revelation 6:9-11; I Cor. 13:12; I Thess. 4:13; Luke 16:23-26; Revelation 21:1-8
3. What do you think the verse in Colossians 3:1 means when it says "set your hearts on things above?"
4. How can you keep from "wasting your pain" and missing an opportunity to help others who may be going through what you have gone through?
4. As you look back through the past chapters what are some of the ways you have seen the author heal from grief? How have you healed or developed in your grief journey?
5. If there was one "take away" you have from the book what would that one thing be for you? Can you think of someone who could benefit from reading this book.

Prayer
Lord, you never promised us that life would be easy. You did promise that you would go be with us as we travel through life. Today I claim your promise that you will never leave or forsake me! Help me Lord to live with an eye toward heaven; my ultimate home. Help me to daily overcome the world and put more of the heavenly things in my life. Teach me Lord God what I must do to prepare us for that grand day in heaven.
'And the very God of peace sanctify you wholly; and I pray God your whole spirit and soul and body be preserved blameless to the coming of our Lord Jesus Christ. Faithful is he that calls you, who also will do it.' –I Thessalonians 5:23-24)

Unison Prayer:
Our Father, which art in heaven. Hallowed be thy Name.
Thy Kingdom come. Thy will be done in earth, As it is in heaven.
Give us this day our daily bread. And forgive us our trespasses, As we forgive them that trespass against us.
And lead us not into temptation, But deliver us from evil. For Thine is the kingdom, The power, and the glory, For ever and ever. Amen.

GUIDELINES FOR USING THE BOOK FOR A SMALL GROUP

This book was written to be used for a small group or class setting. At the end of every chapter is a Study Guide section for accomplishing this purpose. Everyone in the class should have their own copy of the book so they can mark, underline, or circle key thoughts and quotes.

Facilitator Guidelines: As the leader, take time to read the book in its entirety before starting the class. Each week prayerfully review the chapter being taught. Ask God to help you apply the story, truths, and biblical passages to help your class receive the best from the lesson. Every class is filled with different needs so rely heavily on the Holy Spirit for guidance. Invite people to stay after the class for talking, sharing, or spiritual needs.

One Hour Session: Each lesson can be broken down into four 15 minutes parts. The Introduction (15 min), Self-Awareness (15 min), Spiritual Awareness (15 min), and Application (15 min). Lesson time allotment may be limited or expanded as needed.

Small Group Session Outline
Introduction: (15 min)
·   Welcome new members to the class.
·   Opening prayer/Worship (you might use a YouTube worship video)
·   Share a summary statement or a few helpful comments about the focus chapter.

Self-Awareness: (15 min)
·   Read the Discussion Question and ask the class to respond
·   Encourage rich discussion, personal sharing, and sharing of their own story
Spiritual Awareness: (15 min)
·   Invite the class to bring their Bibles to search the scriptures
·   Walk through the biblical scripture references and questions for digging deeper

- Add your own scripture verses that might help the class dig deeper

Application: (15 min)
- Ask the class the following questions as appropriate and time allows:
  o What has God taught you through this week's lesson?
  o What is the big "take away" for this week?
  o What will you do about what you have learned?
  o How can you help someone who might need this truth?
- Try to engage the whole class in applying the truths to their life.
- Encourage the group to think of at least one person they might invite to join the class next week.

- Close the class with prayer and encourage those who want to talk or pray to remain.

Class Options: The book can be used for 12 lessons over a 12 week period. Or, you may shorten the class by a two chapter per week class. If the shorter option is chosen the facilitator will need to choose carefully which questions to use for the more intense six week option.

Biographical information about the author:

Daniel A. Berry

The author was born on April 26, 1953 in Nassawadox, Virginia. He graduated from United Wesleyan College in Allentown, PA.(B.S.), Evangelical School of Theology (MDiv) and Drew University (DMin). He has served as a local church pastor of small, medium, and large sizes over 15 years of pastoral ministry. Recently he has served for the past 14 years as a district superintendent for The Wesleyan Church. In this role he has led over 200 pastors and thousands of local church leaders. His greatest joy is found in developing, resourcing, and consulting with local churches.

He is the proud parent of two sons who are graduates of IWU and serve the local church as a minister and a dentist. They both have a deep love for God that has been passed along to their children.

On September 10, 2007 the author's life changed forever. His wife Shelley and he had a critical car accident. The accident left him with a broken pelvis, ribs and concussion. Shelley was in a coma for three months and was left disabled with a traumatic brain injury. He cared for her while continuing to do ministry.

He continues to serve the local church as a district superintendent and equipper of pastors. Thought his life has been forever changed he constantly prays that he can use his pain to advance the grace and ministry of Jesus Christ.

Selected Bibliography:

Chapter 1:
Dictionary – Britannica – Merriam Webster - http://www.merriam-webster.com/dictionary/grief
Switzer, David K. Pastoral Care Emergencies. Minneapolis: Fortress Press, 2000.
Chapter 2:
Wikipedia. The Matrix - http://en.wikipedia.org/wiki/The_Matrix
Chapter 3:
Dobson, James. When God Doesn't Make Sense. Tyndale Publisher, reprint 2012
Koshner, Harold. When Bad Things Happen to Good People. Anchor Publisher, 2004
Chapter 4:
Swindoll, Charles. Three Steps Forward Two Steps Back. Thomas Nelson Pub., 1998
Guiglio, Louie. "The Megaphone of Hope" – Part Two - http://store.northpoint.org/hope-when-life-hurts-most-part-two-the-megaphone-of-hope.html
Chapter 5:
Chapter 6:
Grief Share. Grief Recovery Support Group Workbook. Church Initiatives. 2006
Chapter 7:
Wright, H. Norman. Experiencing Grief. B & H Books, 2004
Lewis, C.S. A Grief Observed. Faber & Faber, 1961
Ashton, Rosemary. Thomas & Jane Carlyle; Portrait of a Marriage. Random House Publishers. 2003
Chapter 8:
Lewis, C.S., A Grief Observed. Harper One. 1961
Morgan, Robert J. The Red Sea Rules. Thomas Nelson Publisher. 2001
Chapter 9:
Kubler-Ross, Elizabeth. On Death and Dying. New York: Macmillan, 1969.

Neff, Miriam. From One Widow to Another: Conversations on the New You. Moody Publishers, Chicago, Illinois. 2009

Chapter 10:
What Psychiatrist Need to Know About Complicated Grief. http://www.ncbi.nlm.nih.gov/pmc/articles/PMC2691160/
Phyllis Kosminsky. Getting Back to Life When Grief Won't Heal. McGraw Hill Publishers, 2007
Gil, Gillian, We Two: Victoria and Albert: Rulers, Partners, Rivals. Ballentine Books, 2009

Chapter 11:
Lewis, C.S., A Grief Observed. Harper One. 1961

Chapter 12:
Alcorn, Randy. Heaven. Tyndale House Pub., 2004
Pollins, Caleb and Steven Conley Sharp. "Faithful to the End." Brooklyn Tabernacle Choir, Album, Love Lead The Way.